A MODEL OF LEADERSHIP

*How to Manage and Lead
in Engineering and Creative Enterprise*

A MODEL OF LEADERSHIP

How to Manage and Lead in Engineering and Creative Enterprise

RANDALL P. VENDETTI

Published by

Techne Synergies
Parsippany, NJ

Published by

Techne Synergies, LLC
P.O. Box 8241
Parsippany, NJ   07054
www.technesynergies.com

ISBN 978-0-9831376-0-3

Library of Congress Control Number: 2010940459

First Edition

12 11 10 9 8 7 6 5 4 3

To Judie, my wife and best friend—

what we knew in our hearts we wanted to be,
we became, and will be always.

CONTENTS

PREFACE

I have attempted to produce something of wisdom that would be of value to the engineer and the technical manager. It is the kind of wisdom I sought as a young engineer, idealistically hoping to change the world one day, and as a young manager of engineering, realistically trying to *survive* the world *each* day. At the time, there were good books on managing from which I picked up ideas and tips, but nothing showed what it meant to lead from an engineering viewpoint. Managing just goes part of the way, not nearly far enough into the personal adventure of those who push technological envelopes or create new products. There is a human story to technical achievement. It is when one leads individuals, not just manages a function, that one is able to go the whole distance in influencing that human story. The wisdom I have attempted to produce with this book is a refined-type of leadership that works well with educated and highly trained professionals.

I see a need in business and industry for a new perception. There is a lack of recognition of the value each individual represents in connection with know-how and core technologies. Although teams are the best way of bringing about new know-how and for providing innovation, teams are still composed of individuals. The individual is the base unit of everything an organization does, from routine work to change. And since leadership is generally viewed in broad terms, terms that do not translate well for the mundane work of everyday, an understanding of how to lead the individual at the working level becomes a pressing matter.

One of the goals of this book is for the individual engineer to create for themselves a new self-image, one where he or she sees themselves stepping into that leadership role. And so, the real need for a new perception lies with engineers, supervisors, and managers responsible for technical individuals. With this new leadership at the working level, the true value of the individual as the base unit of technology emerges without question, since the only place the organization's know-how can reside is in their heads, and the only way know-how can express itself is by their hands—leaving their hearts the only place over which the leader holds sway.

Another area where a new perception is needed is in that of risk and uncertainty. Looking at the history of technical progress, it is one of individuals without an undue fear of failure. A freedom to fail implies a freedom to try, and it is a trying built upon a past storehouse of lessons from past failures, a process not dissimilar to evolution of living species. No one wants to fail at their endeavors, losing investments and prestige, so it is only right to do all in our power to guarantee success through risk management, but it must be built into the change process at the lowest working level possible, woven into the fabric of the technical effort itself. The individuals from whom we ask for innovation cannot provide for us unless creating something new is blended with the constructive uses of chance and creativity; both are not the places to be paralyzed by a fear of failure and an aversion to trying.

In this book, I offer a model of leadership which simplifies that which is complex—a simple model of a complex reality. What I present is not intended to be an exhaustive work on the subject, or a piece from academic research, but rather a boiling down to the essence of how to lead beyond the classic management techniques readily available. The model is not intended to be a step-by-step procedure, nor is it, but a mnemonic as an aid for the practicing engineer, supervisor, or manager in touching all the points required for positively interacting and influencing an individual for whom they are responsible. In addition to the model, I present basic principles, each overarching to the model. The model of leadership can be the foundation for developing a personal leadership philosophy and style. The foundation can be added to in order to make the leadership edifice larger or stronger, but be careful removing any portion of the basic foundation.

The engineering profession tells a story of how an older engineer who is traveling in the wilderness is asked why he is wasting time and effort building a bridge across a chasm where he had just crossed. He replies, "it is for those who follow after me, for you see, starting long ago others who came before me over similar chasms built bridges for *me*." This book is my attempt at a bridge. If just one person crosses, it has served its purpose.

Randall P. Vendetti
Parsippany, NJ
September 2010

CHAPTER *1*

INTRODUCTION TO A REFINED LEADERSHIP

"Not in their application, certainly, but their principles you may; to learn is not to know; there are the learners and the learned. Memory makes the one, philosophy the other."

"... for there are two distinct sorts of ideas, those that proceed from the head and those that emanate from the heart."

Abbe' Faria to Edmond Dantès,
from Alexandre Dumas, The Count of Monte Cristo[1]

This is a book for engineers, for managers of technical professionals, and for those aspiring to become managers. It is a book that may be of interest to executives whose businesses require innovative outcomes. In general, it is a book for people who need to accomplish difficult tasks that have no clear solutions, and for those who need to bring about something, functioning as intended, from nothing. But above all, this book is for anyone needing to bridge the difference between managing in the form of direct control and that of managing in the form of an inspiring leadership.

Engineers and other technical professionals in companies producing technical products or offering a technical service usually take the lead for projects or teams. In addition, departmental managers in these companies usually come up from the ranks of engineers. Mustering, organizing, and directing resources to accomplish objectives is not difficult for someone with an engineering background. These tasks require clear, analytical thinking, usually a strong point for engineers. The fact an engineer would have completed complicated projects and would have solved many difficult problems before becoming a manager would testify to this ability. The engineer is prepared for the new responsibilities of manager with skills associated with rationality, objectivity, and precision—only now these skills are to be applied at a higher level and with more impact for the organization. These tools are still necessary, but they fall short of being sufficient to serve the new manager. New tools and different ways of thinking and acting are needed by the technical manager not just for managing on a technical basis, but also for leading people. These are quite two different activities and mind-sets.

A common failing of the engineer as manager, or an engineer leading a team, is the inability to let go of performing and controlling the technical work, and the inability to not treat his or her reports as extensions of himself or herself. Those who suffer from this, at a minimum, constrain growth and deprive opportunity for both the organization and the technical professionals for whom the engineer, or manager, is responsible. At worst, the engineer opens up possibilities for direct failure by not obtaining business objectives. A manager, or team leader, is on the wrong track who feels the way to manage is by using people to amplify his or her own talents and drive, his or her own beliefs and experiences, and his or her own approach to work. This kind of thinking is limiting and is blind to the immense possibilities beyond the limits of that manager, and the limits of his or her knowledge and abilities. Even if the individual manager is *the* expert in a particular field, prodigious in accomplishment, there exists a limit at which point the manager becomes a bottleneck, a force that holds back the organization, and is no longer effective. One individual is not scalable for unconstrained creative accomplishment in a business, or for growth of that business; however, add individuals with organization and true leadership, then any scale is possible. This is not to say for a manager all that is needed is to organize, assign, and delegate; something more is needed. One cannot put people on autopilot, type in the parameters for the course, and then walk away. The leader finds an optimal level of involvement, staying attuned with them, and understanding deeply the circumstances surrounding them and their projects.

Where routine is prevalent in the work, and little is expected or pursued in the way of new products, new processes, or new markets, deficiencies in leadership skills of the manager are not acutely felt in terms of the organization's continuance. Even with continuous, incremental improvement of current operations associated with routine processes, skills required of the manager are analytical in nature, focusing on efficiency. But in today's world of business, especially for engineers and other technical personnel working in industry, change is the order of business, not routine; effectiveness is needed, not efficiency. If nothing else, modern business is the challenge of constant conceptual change, and that requires skills for the leadership of the individual on the working level.

The heart of this book is based on a model of leadership that shows the working parts of how to extend managing into leading. Although they have in common getting things done through others, there is a difference. Managing is expected to be precise with solutions, whereas leading conjures up going down new paths that are not clear, requiring solutions with no one right answer. Both need a large dose of judgment and concern for risk and uncertainty. But leading involves, to a larger extent, an uncertain future.

A leader, going beyond managing, accounts for the expanded capabilities and larger capacity of others for whom he or she is responsible, and has the ability to energize those capabilities and that capacity. With such, the leader and the organization will experience good outcomes that no one could have predicted, controlled, or imagined, leaving one smiling all day. By embracing uncertainty and its association with people and events, one reduces risk, and can even go so far as to use the unexpected to one's advantage.

From this point on, I will write in first and second person, from me to you. It will be personal, as it should be with the type of close-up leadership that is being presented. This book is the result of years of experience and lessons learned, of formal education, of keeping up with the literature and news, and mostly of deep thinking. But the real knowledge comes from introspection after my applying the ideas that have now found their way into this book to the day-to-day management of engineering projects, groups, and departments for over thirty years. Much of the ideas and statements in this book can be corroborated as valuable by anyone with exposure to the workings within a manufacturing or service company, within an engineering group, or within a research laboratory. I do not intend for this book to be an academic work, only a "how to" book on practical, but not always obvious, matters.

Believing in yourself, as most successful engineers do, is not enough, but believing in others is from where the true magic comes. By your leadership, not only can you bring out the best in individuals for whom you are responsible, but also the best in individuals with whom you work, inside and outside the organization. The approach presented will help you reach an uncustomary style of leadership compared to what is commonly found in the workplace today, setting you apart, and contributing to your advantage and to that of your firm. This style of leadership fits nicely with the trends in social networking and the emergence of interactive and adaptive Web-based communities where no one is in control. It may be a good approach to leadership for the new, distributed, global enterprise.

A WORD OVER-USED

The word *leadership* can have many meanings. To compound the matter further, it is a word which is overused and, to my way of thinking, worn out. There are many books on leadership based on almost every historical person of significance. They are all instructive, having a common thread of knowing how to work with people, understanding and using human nature, and not trying to change that nature. On the other hand, there is a popular notion of leader who provides all the answers, whose approval is required on everything, and the one who takes charge, that is, a leadership style that gets things done despite human nature. This type of leader fits the leader-of-the-pack model of command-and-control, being a dominating force, and being personally domineering. The word leadership can take you in two different directions.

I was recently at a conference on leadership, and it turned out to be focused on leading large, global organizations. What struck me the most was how the words associated with leadership being spoken lost all meaning by being distant from what mattered on the working level of the organization. When put at such lofty levels, even the most important words become platitudes. How can this tendency of such an important subject becoming trite be reversed? This can be done by applying any concepts personally on a human level of daily contact; then words associated with leadership become powerful again—and stay powerful. On a working level, interacting with the doers, seeing the detail and the moving parts, a person obtains a deeper understanding of the subject, making leadership a meaningful and a useful word.

I tried finding a substitute word not yet overused, avoiding the word *leadership*. You can see my success with that. Instead, I have added the adjective *refined*. This I hope will distinguish the kind of leadership required of a leader in engineering and a creative enterprise from that of a leader-of-the-pack in command and in control.

WHAT IS MEANT BY "REFINED"

What type of leadership style brings out the best in highly-trained, inventive, and knowledge-based workers? My experiences suggest it is not an approach similar to being in command and control, nor being a taskmaster, and it is something quite different from micromanaging every detail. Counterintuitively, the performance of technical people is affected by their emotion and by drawing on their uniqueness, especially when at the edge, pushing the boundaries of a technical and entrepreneurial envelope. About getting good results from people whose work has any creative content, I assure you the process and performance will be affected by the degree of freedom each individual has in utilizing their different talents and backgrounds. Leading such workers, besides managing the precise technical aspects of their job, requires a refinement in style that encompasses and allows for a better and unique understanding of each individual; it requires providing meaning for each individual for why they are there at work; it requires helping them with their standing in the organization; and it is consistently tied together with what is intrinsic to all of us, our human nature.

Engineers know the truth of Francis Bacon's famous quote: "Nature, to be commanded, must be obeyed." He meant this for physical phenomenon, but I contend that it applies to human nature as well. Any process, procedure, law, or practice, that goes against human nature is destined to not function well, if it were to function at all. David Hume's "Nature is always too strong for principle" suggests it is always better not to use your limited energy on wishful thinking or unsound practice, and never on trying to overcome the nature of how things operate. A refined leader is a student of how people work and of how to work well with people.

You cannot see inside a worker's head, so you cannot see what is actually going on with the work. You cannot see how your latest interaction with an individual affected for good or ill the work's progress. Yes, you can see results once they materialize along the way, but you cannot see the waste that occurred in getting there; and, you cannot see what might have been. I speculate that there are historically countless thousands of good ideas, methods, and products for thousands of companies, that might have been, but were not, causing stunted growth, financial loss, and even failure. One could never be sure how a given company succeeded from just one idea that started out fragile, needing the room to grow in the heads of its technical people, unseen by management. A refined leadership attuned with, and accommodating for, the individual and the team will realize new ideas for competitive advantage of the business—the business as is, or itself as changed by the resultant creativity from this style of leadership.

When you use refined leadership, you keep the working environment emotionally positive, going out of your way not to create the existence of fear, uncertainty, distain, or distrust. One way to shut down the higher functioning of the brain, and with it initiative and creativity, is by triggering the primitive functions in humans through negative emotions, such as by fear activating personal defense mechanisms. Think back to a time when you were preoccupied emotionally by fear or anger. Were you able to focus your thoughts, or to think creatively, or even to be inspired to push on?

A working environment may not have a negative feel, but almost as bad, it may have no feel, lacking excitement and spirit. When asking the individual to do more, encouraging them to go beyond the safe harbor of just doing what they feel comfortable doing, the refined leader must create the atmosphere that inspires individuals and teams to be more by envisioning more. All this comes from focusing on the individual, what is important to them, and what it means to them to succeed in the trial confronting them. Refined leadership allows others to be, and lets them know they are, the center of the action; and by this, boredom and tedium during waking hours are replaced by excitement and spirit.

A refined leader is subtle and seamlessly works into the context of the situation what is required by way of interaction—unless a constructive purpose is served by being dramatic and obvious. The positive influence is behind the scenes, and at times invisible, letting individuals and teams be in control and self-directed. There is no place for self-promotion by the manager over that of individuals and teams. The refined leader lets individuals be in the spotlight. Overt control and self-promotion not only weakens the leader in the eyes of others, it is an act of trying to diminish the stature of individuals being led. Subtlety means one does not control by demonstrative instruction, but by standards and fellowship.

The following summarizes what is and what is not meant by refined leadership in a work environment:

Refined leadership *is* ...

- Consistent with human nature
- Tactful and professional, yet engaging and energizing
- Always positive and constructive
- Bringing out the best in people, encouraging their growth
- Subtle, not obvious, seamlessly worked into situation
- Behind the scenes, putting others in spotlight
- Setting up workable situations

Refined leadership *is not* ...

- Command-and-control
- Dominating or domineering
- Imposing undue restrictions and constraints
- Creating or using a negative feel, or ignoring emotion as a factor
- Concern for self-promotion
- Conceit that is never wrong, and knows better than others

In the area of objectives and strategy, a refined leader looks to set up the individual for a high probability, or at least for the possibility, of success. He or she does not expect from, or demand of, the individual to make right an unfeasible project or unworkable situation. When you practice refined leadership, make sure you think through what you are asking the individual to do. Determine for yourself whether it could be done at all and the degree of difficulty.

A SPECIAL CASE OF LEADERSHIP

A managing engineer, or a manager of a technical function, is faced with two opposites of nature: precision and exactitude in the physical world vs. obscurity and nebulousness in the world of people.

Within the overall category of leadership, going beyond managing into leadership in engineering emerges as a special case of leadership. It is a case where a duality exists. On the one side of the duality, the technical manager must deal with concrete technical matters. With this, a strict conformance to universal physical laws is required for products to function well, if at all. On the other side, the technical manager encounters quite the opposite where people are concerned, dealing with people as individuals, groups, and teams with the attendant interactions of personalities, emotions, and thinking. On this side of the duality, knowing how to obtain good results requires understanding people, what they are made of, what they can do, and what they care about. Mere technical knowledge and skill that may be enough for a task oriented boss, or an efficient supervisor, is not enough for the engineering manager who leads.

In addition to the two extremes of the physical world and the people world, there are the differences between two kinds of work. The first is doing that which has been done many times before, and doing this work well and efficiently. It pertains to work content that has become routine and performed through standard processes. The second is doing that which has never been done before and is new. It pertains to work content that is being changed or created, and it involves innovation. In this second kind of work, the physical world and the people world meet, forming somewhat of a weather front, upsetting organizational and marketplace equilibrium.

Also, the special case of leadership stems from a need to simultaneously reconcile all the realities just mentioned above with the practical demands required of a successful business. It especially comes into stark relief when the engineering manager is responsible for creating something new, in the area of change and innovation. With this, imagination, nonconformance, and messiness take over, but the need for getting the technical part right still remains. Here, no-nonsense precise analysis resulting in only one right answer co-exists with imprecise imaginative solutions with *many* right answers that at times comes about *through* nonsense.

The people side of the duality is not easy for a strong-willed, knowledgeable, and accomplished engineer in a managing role. The engineering manager is expected to have all the answers, however, a refined engineering leader allows others to have most of the answers, to do the work, to get the credit, and to grow as a result—all without the engineer leader feeling threatened or vulnerable. Managers are not leading when they withhold authority, independence, and power, making the individual feel less important in their own eyes and in the eyes of others; however, this is the tendency when so much is on the line for the engineering manager.

Adding to its special case of leadership, the engineer uses a kind of creativity that is different from that of the artist, or what is generally regarded by society as being creative. (I once had an acquaintance tell me that so-and-so was creative, unlike me since I was an engineer. At that point, I realized that most people do not know what engineers do.) The results of technical creativity is valued based on the degree of fitness for a purpose or for satisfying an objective at hand—not just for art's sake. What is more, this creativity results in concrete technical ideas and actions, conforms to natural laws and business realities, and succeeds by satisfying market needs.

A SUITABLE PERSONALITY

You may be thinking an obstacle and a big issue with engineers and other technical professionals as leaders is their stereotypical personality of being introverted. I do not know whether engineers as a group are more introverted compared to other professions, such as law, medicine, or accounting. I do believe it is true when compared with entertainers and sales people; it is *because* of their outgoing nature they choose these professions. But I have good news, you do not have to change your personality to be a leader, especially to that of the entertainer's or salesperson's love of theater.

By the way, the root for the word *theater* is Greek for see, view, or behold. It is interesting that for the word *theory* the root is similar, it is Greek for spectator. With theater, it is how you are *viewed by others*, their perception of you, but most importantly, their response to you. As with theory, it is how things and people are *viewed by you*, resulting in a mental model or world view, and a philosophy for your thinking and actions. I contend the province of a refined leader is equally how you view the world (theory), affecting your actions, and how the world perceives you (theater), affecting responses to you. Both make up the subject of this book.

I remember a cartoon in a newspaper. Standing and facing each other were two research-type looking men, both in lab coats and holding clipboards. The physical features of the one speaking and his body language, such as a sad-sack face and looking down at the floor, suggested shyness and the personality of an introvert. This person was assuring the other that he was a people person, and all that the other person had to do was go and ask his people. At first, I could not put my finger on why this was funny, even though it was funny to me. If you were speaking to a true people person, it would be obvious to you. One would think that you being a person—the object of his or her strength—you would not need proof other than interacting with him or her. That got me thinking, if a person were to consider themselves a process person, you would look to the processes that that person used. If a person considered themselves a results person, you would look to the results that that person achieved. Therefore, if a person considered themselves a leader, you would look to the individuals whom that person positively influenced. So maybe the second person in the cartoon *should* go ask the people.

I find interacting with and positively influencing people can be easy when it is a matter of working toward a common purpose. For instance, an entertainer's introversion would be of no consequence if the focus were on exercising their skill through their craft. The entertainer relates to the audience through the common purpose of the show, and that same entertainer might feel awkward meeting people from the audience after the show. When there is an object to your interaction with someone, then you do not have to worry about small talk, or finding a topic to discuss, as in social situations. Focusing on the business at hand in a work situation will provide enough to talk about. Of course, you will need to consider building rapport with the other person. This is covered later in the book.

Although you do not have to change your personality to be a leader, you do have to change your actions and thinking with respect to people. The *refined leadership model* presented later shows in what areas and how you can have a positive effect on people in a work setting, especially on those for whom you are responsible or with whom you work closely.

POTENCY OF LEADER WITH TECHNICAL KNOWLEDGE

None of the discussions surrounding managing and leadership imply you should give up your thinking or acting as an engineer, or technical specialist, when needed and appropriate. Here lies your advantage over those who are non-technical in management or leadership roles in technical organizations. You can derive even more benefit from refined leadership of engineers and technical professionals with the added help of your good technical understanding of the work being performed. In addition, you have the ability, when suitable for your organization, to blend that leadership with the practice of your professional discipline. However, guard against the pitfalls already presented of not putting those for whom you are responsible first. You must find the optimum blend for a given situation. At times you will perform as pure leader and at other times as pure engineer, but most of the time you will perform in some proportion as both.

The extent to which you leave the technical work to others is determined by the size of the group for which you are responsible and your level in the organization. A supervisor of two people, for example, will have a larger portion of the work he or she performs be technical as compared to an engineering manager of twenty people; and a vice president of engineering with the responsibility of fifty people will perform much less direct technical work, if any at all.

In crisis mode, you will find paradoxically that you will need to be both more a leader and more an engineer, that is, you will do more of both even though the proportion of technical to non-technical may be the same. This is possible by increasing your activity level higher than is sustainable for only short periods, and spending more time than usual to focus intently on the problem. Leadership skills, or the lack of those skills, are keenly apparent in a crisis.

An individual contributor in an organization has the best opportunity to perform both the work of their technical specialty and that of their role as leader. When managing a project or leading a project team, influencing the team members to become a high performing team is paramount to good technical outcomes. As a team member, the engineer can step up where needed to fill a leadership role, which may not only benefit the team and the organization, but will help the individual be recognized for those abilities. If this is the case for you, then the model of leadership can give you the confidence that you are addressing all the right areas for people leadership.

ONE MODEL AND A NUMBER OF OVERARCHING PRINCIPLES

I formulated a simple method that relates the people oriented elements of leadership with the more familiar analytical aspects of managing. I present refined leadership in the form of a graphical model. Using a graphical representation is suitable for engineers and other technical professionals since they are accustomed to seeing complex ideas expressed in diagrammatical form. By representing leadership this way, technical professionals will see the elegant simplicity of connecting all the elements that make leadership what it is.

You can use the model of leadership as a learning aid; later you can use it as a mnemonic to recall and apply the ideas when working with people day-to-day. Starting from this model, you can continue the development of your particular style of leadership that fits the specific kind of technical work and organization in which you are involved. Over time, your style should evolve from lessons you continually learn in your career as you apply these ideas to managing and leading.

The model of leadership pertains to each individual for whom you have responsibility or with whom you have need to interact on projects or teams. This is important to remember: one model is a snapshot in time for one individual. So if you should have five people reporting to you as a manager, or five team members working with you as a team leader, then you should apply five models to the five individuals, that is, one model per individual.

The following is an overview of the model of leadership. At the model's core is JOB. You can think of JOB as the embodiment of a position description for a particular situation in the organization for an individual. JOB is the province of the technical manager, where in the strictest sense the analytically oriented skills of *managing only* are necessary and somewhat sufficient. An extreme and stereotypical example of JOB is the function of a clerk in a bureaucracy doing the same thing in the same way, everyday. Efficiency is associated with JOB, and the need to keep things flowing by performing the tasks required for the daily operation of the organization.

Interlacing with and extending beyond JOB, the model adds the components of an individual's SUBSTANCE and STATURE. These two qualitative characteristics within an organization are normally connected to each other by JOB. To demonstrate how this works, say an individual engineer who reports to you may have immense SUBSTANCE as a human being. He has internally high standards and cares deeply, and has a strong and diverse background. Also, as part of SUBSTANCE, this individual, as does every individual, has knowledge, skills, and judgment over and above what is needed for performing in JOB. However, this same individual in the example, because of factors such as poor or no reputation, lack of past success and types of projects, and no authority, may lack STATURE in the organization. He does not have a freedom to act or a recognized importance in the organization, and he does not have power to get things done. This mis-match of SUBSTANCE and STATURE will keep the individual from higher levels of performance in the organization and may cause internal and external conflicts for the individual. It is also an area on which you as leader can focus; the gap between SUBSTANCE and STATURE may keep the individual from performing their best in JOB.

The refined leader is the one to influence positive changes for the individual, if needed, in JOB, SUBSTANCE, and STATURE. This is done through the next component of the model of leadership, that is, through providing MEANING. MEANING is based on the leader's relationship with the individual and the creation of immediate purpose—the reason both of you are there to begin with, doing what you are doing. Immediate purpose is related to the individual's contribution to the organization. Incorporated in the purpose you create for the individual is business vision and the higher purpose of the organization, especially the benefits provided to people and society by doing one's job.

The leadership components of SUBSTANCE, STATURE, and MEANING overlap and extend managing beyond the component of JOB. Additionally, for the individual to grow and for the organization to innovate, the area of JOB widens into that of CHALLENGE. CHALLENGE is another component upon which the refined leader has influence. In the area of CHALLENGE, the influence extends beyond the individual, indirectly affecting teams and groups for better outcomes. The key areas for this influence will be in that which is unexplored associated with products, processes, and technologies, with the operation of chance, and with the use of creativity. Risk and uncertainty is addressed in CHALLENGE. In the realm of CHALLENGE, the individual creates something new or different, and does it in a new way. Where efficiency is associated with JOB, effectiveness is associated with CHALLENGE.

Chapter 3, *The Model*, begins the detail presentation of the refined leadership model. The model components of MEANING, CHALLENGE, SUBSTANCE, JOB, and STATURE will be broken down to workable model elements. Chapters following Chapter 3 will be dedicated to each of these components of the model.

Everybody will take away different wisdom from the leadership model and what I present in this book. I hope a particular philosophy of leadership will emerge for you. Your leadership should fit into the bigger picture of the workings of your organization. The application of these ideas and techniques to suit the varied situations you encounter will take practice, and any mental and physical energy expended by you in this area can only make you stronger as a leader of people.

In addition to the graphical representation of the refined leadership model, I offer twenty-two *Overarching Principles*. Important concepts are distilled into a few good rules expressed as principles in the form of key statements; they are intersperse throughout the book in the appropriate section. Compare them with what you know and use them to perform thought experiments by considering their validity. Hopefully, as you test their validity, separately and working in combination, you go beyond what is stated in these principles to a higher level of awareness about leadership.

Understanding, and the process by which one comes to understand, is the subject of the next chapter. The ideas on understanding override any other consideration in working with the leadership model. Without it, good judgment is not possible, decisions are not effective, and situations are left confused. If you were to get nothing from this book other than the lessons from Chapter 2, *Understanding, Before All Else,* then I would consider it worth the effort.

UNDERSTANDING, BEFORE ALL ELSE

"The best expedient to prevent this confusion, is to be modest in our preten-sions; and even to discover the difficulty ourselves before it is objected to us. By this means, we may make a kind of merit of our very ignorance."

David Hume, An Enquiry Concerning Human Understanding[1]

O nce a young development engineer ask me how I came to make a decision that resolved an entangled affair. It involved per-sonal conflict between two individuals that was entwined with a number of project issues. I was not sure how to answer him. I knew it had to do with proceeding with the confidence that I *could* find a solution; the kind of confidence that comes from having solved simi-lar problems in the past. I knew it had to do with finding as many facts about the situation as possible; the best facts coming from peo-ple involved first-hand, or by my direct observations. However, facts and observations are not enough, it had to do with seeking opinions from others on possible causes and solutions to the problem. I knew it had to do with deep thinking on the subject. I knew judgment was involved; judgment being the one essential ingredient in good decision making. After these ideas flashed before me, I wanted to be dramatic with a succinct philosophical answer; one that would condense all the above into a nice, neat statement.

I offered him what I knew to be the crux of my process, and thus possibly a universal method to solve just such a problem as the personal conflict with project issues. The answer had to do with understanding the issue from all angles, and considering all the facts and opinions. So there it was, my dramatic, succinct, philosophical answer: understand! The response I gave him that day I made into Overarching Principle #1:

Overarching Principle #1:

Make every effort to understand, then decide and act; but first, fully understand.

This is not a new idea. Bias of Priene, one of the Seven Wise Men of Greece, around the sixth century BC stated "Know and then act." Winston Churchill uttered similar words, with his "Ponder, then act." However, pondering is the act of thinking. It implies trying to understand, but it does not explicitly state it. "Know" implies understanding, but it seems static to me, relating to facts. By using the word understand in the principle, it states the ultimate need of not just knowing the facts, but also of comprehending the implications of those facts.

The use of Overarching Principle #1 must always be active with you. In applying the refined leadership model that will be presented in detail in the next chapter, you will need to use your skills in understanding when addressing each element of the model.

Understanding cannot be obtained by thinking only, although it is an important ingredient. You will have to do fact finding using a number of methods. Inquiring and having dialogue with the appropriate people is one method. Through this important activity, together you explore facts, implications, and possible solutions, while obtaining the opinions of people directly or indirectly involved. This collaborative effort helps the most for understanding, since the experiences and the world views of many can be brought to bear on an issue, with you as a clearinghouse, helping you make reasonably good conclusions derived from the process to understand.

IN THE PROCESS OF UNDERSTANDING

The following are approaches you can use to help you come to understand any situation better. Depending on circumstances, you can use one at a time, or a number in combination. You will find you cannot help but use a number simultaneously.

- Change from answer-provider to question-asker
- Doubt your mental model and underlying assumptions
- Do not be overconfident in what you know
- Inquire of others to expand awareness
- Observe first-hand
- Go from bottom-up vs. top-down
- Look deeper, when all goes well
- Ask why, when anything goes poorly

Using in practice each approach to understand will allow them to become second nature to you. You will then have the ability to use each technique, separately or in combination, smoothly, seam-lessly, and subtly.

Change from answer-provider to question-asker

To understand a situation deeply and fully, you are required to ask difficult, powerful, and enlightening questions. For someone with a background in engineering, this changes one's default role from the traditional answer-provider to question-asker. An engineer, or other technical professional, who has worked for a length of time in areas such as design, research, analysis, studies, fabrication, or construc-tion most likely has been an answer-provider. This is the basis of the the phenomenon of what I call *the answer man*. With this phenome-non, you are looked upon as having any and all answers to whatever question anyone thinks you should have the answers to, and you have subconsciously accepted this. An engineer's role of having the answers becomes ingrained and habitual with everyone in the or-ganization. This phenomenon could put you in a frame of mind that could short-circuit the process of arriving at full understanding when it is most needed.

I am sure you have experienced the answer man phenomenon before, maybe once, or more than once. It may have been in a meet-ing where someone from marketing, production, management, or possibly a customer, turned to you with a difficult question. Now, if you happened not to have the answer to that question, and the setting was conducive to grandstanding by the questioner, then you were suddenly on the hot seat. The tone of the questioner might have be-come moralizing, "why *don't* you know?" or "*shouldn't* you know?" The more penetrating the questions and the harder they were to an-swer, the more lopsided the perception became that somehow the questioner was more informed of the situation, was more aware of the implications to the business, and cared more than you. Others may have even piled on at your expense. After each encounter like this, you vowed never to not know the unknowable again. Once again, the self-image of the engineer was subconsciously reinforced as one of answer-provider, and not question-asker.

This phenomenon of the answer-provider being the one who should know all the answers has the opposite effect. The answer-provider can never say "I don't know," the beginning of learning something new. The answer man is kept from learning by openly questioning, especially when it makes them appear not to know what they should know. In addition, this phenomenon leads those in the engineering function in organizations from having the belief that it is their place to question, especially questions pertaining to the larger picture addressed to those in authority or non-technical functions.

To find deep understanding before deciding and acting, you as technical leader, and those for whom you have responsibility, must change roles when appropriate from answer-provider to question-asker. Of course, you still need to provide answers to do your work as an engineer, but now they are balanced by your asking difficult, powerful, and enlightening questions that are needed for deeper un-derstanding.

Doubt your mental model and underlying assumptions

With a catastrophic collapse of, say, a bridge or a financial system, beforehand there was a firm mind-set of the practitioner. This mind-set came about partially from formal knowledge, partially from tacit assumptions, and partially from not considering possibilities that were unimagined. Examples of such unimagined possibilities for a bridge may be the dynamics of wind forces, and for a financial sys-tem, drastically falling home prices. Over time, assumptions and the system of thought itself are accepted as valid beyond doubt. At that point, even the conditions at the boundaries upon which a model of thought is constructed are overlooked, or just plain forgotten in application.

There are many examples of disasters in history resulting from erroneous, tacit mental models, with bad assumptions or ignored constraints. Calamities have a way of changing the mind-set, or the paradigm, of an industry or a company. You do not want to wait for a disaster to re-evaluate your approach. By viewing it in another way, you can perform what is commonly referred to as a sanity check. Do these other perspectives confirm the validity of your approach?

Better understanding requires you to modify your mental model, or world view, as an on-going exercise. To do this, find the weaknesses of your approach or argument using a different perspective. Try to look at the issue from the viewpoint of others. Try to imagine the adverse consequences of a decision or course of action. What is it that can go wrong that you do not want to go wrong? Do thought experiments by subjecting the model to the utmost extreme conditions and ask yourself what would happen at those extremes. Ask a lot of *what if* questions.

As with the first method for understanding, find and ask difficult questions to expose your weakest and untenable underlying assumptions. This should not only be for technical, but also nontechnical matters. These techniques overlap into the area of creativity where one needs to overcome unconscious mental constraints, or fictitious restrictions, those that cause blockage to one's expansive thinking. The restrictions that the thinker unknowingly imposes on himself or herself is covered in Chapter 5, *Spirit of Challenge*, under the sections for Chance and Creativity.

Do not be overconfident in what you know

Most technical professionals are, or have been, an expert in one or more specialties. With that expertise comes the focus of a specialist, which is a good thing, except when it interferes with broader under-standing. If you were to be a specialist, or were to have a number of specialists for whom you are responsible in your organization, then beware of the focus of the specialist in the form of tunnel vision. Tunnel vision is seeing only what you focus on, and nothing more. I was watching two snorkelers in the water while I was on a beach re-cently. They were using diving masks and snorkels, swimming slowly, looking for interesting fish. I spotted a large, ominous, dark mass just under the surface of the water swimming passed them on their left side. I thought the mass was going to hit them, it was that close. I wanted to yell out to them, but at that distance and underwa-ter they would not have heard me. Do you think they saw this ma-rine creature that passed by, almost hitting them? No, they did not turn their heads; instead, they were focused looking for interesting fish where they saw them before, straight down. This is a good ex-ample of tunnel vision, where one sees too narrowly, focusing in-tently elsewhere while the object of that focus swims by unnoticed.

Experts tend to come to conclusions based on the content of their past knowledge and past results of cause and effect, rather than by an open process of learning anew. Experts and specialists run into trouble because they rely too heavily on past solutions. The ex-pert is inclined to believe he or she is on the right course, and sees no need to expend time and money considering anything outside what is known to be right.

How can you avoid the pitfalls of focusing too finely, of tun-nel vision? You, and those individuals for whom you are ultimately responsible, can consciously make a point to look around, away from the object of your focus, now and then. Do this by first admitting you may not have the right answers from past experience, and then by using the approaches provided for arriving at a better understanding. Also, actively look for feedback and criticism, and include individuals on teams that have new and different perspectives.

Specialized experience should be an asset, and it could be if you were to continually broaden your understanding of the situation and the surrounding circumstances. Whatever the endeavor, you should not assume all will go well just because you have done it before. Yes, uncertainty goes down as the task becomes more routine, but the risk increases from a fixed mind-set. Do not become overconfident with past formulas of success.

Inquire of others to expand awareness

You can expand awareness by seeing things from different angles, that is, from the vantage of different perspectives and interests. A good technique is to take on the task for yourself of reconciling points of view from many people with a stake and an interest in a given situation. By trying to find a solution to the puzzle of satisfying everyone, you force yourself to see from the perspective of each. Finding a solution that fits, technical or non-technical, requires knowing increasingly more detail and the many difficulties of all parts of the situation. This is why a cross-functional team is effective and valuable to a company. By design, it has people from all the affected functions of the organization, assuring all perspectives are considered. Later in the book I cover teams, an important part of the effectiveness of refined leadership.

Learn how to listen; do not be the talker all the time. I have a favorite method of learning and understanding from others, especially from those whom I am responsible. I sit down with one or two individuals, usually at a conference table in my office. I find one-on-one is best, but more than one is alright when the situation calls for it. I close the door and try to create a relaxed atmosphere. It feels as if the problems are outside, and we have time to discuss things quietly for a period out of the storm. With a clean sheet of paper in front of me and my pen in hand, we dive into our discussion. First, the individual tells the story of what is happening, the problems, the breakthroughs, the next steps, the risks and uncertainties, anything the individual wants to tell me. This works due to mutual truthfulness and trust. I ask technical and non-technical questions, striving to understand as much as I can. All during this time I am jotting notes; this is important because you will forget details that you will need later, but most of all, by this action you let the individual know that what he or she is saying is important.

When inquiring of others to expand awareness in this way, you are not only understanding more by seeing through eyes of others and by their opinions, but you are working on relationships. Whenever you can, you should be collaborating with others, working closely toward common purpose. The benefits of this approach cannot be overstated.

Observe first-hand

To discern what others do not, or cannot, is the object of taking a look for yourself. Even if another were to explain accurately what they saw, it would not be possible to provide the preciseness and the extent needed by you for picking out an idea generating detail or for making a connection that only you in your unique position could catch. This is true for you and for those for whom you are responsible. In addition, observing first-hand is a good way for personally obtaining objective evidence, unfiltered by opinion and bias. The popular idea of *management by walking around* has first-hand observation as one of its benefits.

Have you ever played the game *Telephone* when you were younger? It is the game where the first person in a long line of people whispers a sentence or phrase into the ear of the second, and the second whispers what they heard into the ear of the third, and so on until the sentence gets to the last person. After the last person says out loud what he or she heard, the first person reveals the sentence or phrase. Everyone is astonished that the two are comically different. This phenomenon operates in real life with large groups. It is always better to hear it directly from the source. The closer someone is to being a first-hand account when informing you of something, the better, if you could not be a witness yourself.

This advice concerning observing first-hand applies equally to technical and people issues. With situations involving people, be careful with what one person says of another, or what the latest rumors are about a particular person. Human beings in the social sphere in organizations are rarely objective. People will form opinions about others quickly. In my experience, after observing first-hand by getting to know a person in question, the opinion I form of that person rarely matches the opinion offered to me by others. Did you ever have a teacher or a professor who you liked, or who was your favorite teacher ever, and before your first class other students said she was the worse teacher, difficult or strict, and you would hate her? With people, form your own opinions first-hand.

In one of my early positions in industry as an engineer, I developed disposable medical products. In a corporate headquarters setting, I obtained ideas from users, applied engineering theory to product design, tested prototypes, all in an atmosphere rich in creativity. When I made my first visit to one of the manufacturing facilities, the manufacturing people joked with me, "here's the young engineer hotshot from corporate." There was a lot of truth to their joking. This young corporate hotshot came away with more information and ideas about the product in the short time I spent with a few line workers than I could have in any length of time back in my corporate cubicle or with my engineering theory. This memory has stuck with me throughout my engineering and management career, goading me to get up from my desk and get out into the action.

Go from bottom-up vs. top-down

For any given topic or matter at hand at any point in time, pick an individual, and they will know more than another. The individual is not smarter, he or she is more cognizant. Cognizance is a state that occurs when one is more aware by being close to a situation, maybe even an actor in the events. Cognizance pertains to the history of decisions and results, of past and current problems, and of what did and did not work as solutions. At any instance, the smallest, intimate detail of knowledge will be known by those who are cognizant.

I recommend you consult with those who are cognizant when seeking and obtaining information, opinions, and decisions. You want to hear it directly from those who actually know. I have experienced the opposite many times, where those in authority, and others, discussing an issue incessantly, unknowingly used wild assumptions, wishful thinking, and strong opinions of little value. They could have saved time and confusion by listening to those who knew the details and finer points, getting to the truth of the matter. They were proceeding from top-down, not bottom-up, when they made their decisions based on partial, and often wrong, understanding.

Start to obtain the facts and specific knowledge from the engineer designing the product, the technician testing the product, the operator running the machine, or the salesperson in front of the customer. A good place to find up-to-date and pertinent information is from the project team, not someone unconnected to the project. Rely more on facts and opinions from individuals who have been hands-on with the situation, not from someone who has not.

Look deeper, when all goes well

Basking in the warmth of success feels good. When things go right, human nature is such that we feel like nothing can go wrong. Isn't this the basis of emotions when investing in the stock market? When stocks are up, maybe up too high, the feeling is good and the belief is they will go up forever. But objectively and through experience, we know better. Do not be the last fool to buy in a euphoric market, and do not be fooled by success in your work when you are feeling good.

Being objective with yourself is the beginning of looking deeper when something is going right. A good way to start is to ask a number of iterations of the question *how* the good outcome was reached. Your goal is to find the root cause of what is going, or has gone, right. You might be surprised. The reason you think all is going well, or went well, may not be the true underlying reason. You may save yourself a different kind of surprise, a potential sudden shift from currently going well to going badly. For more on negative events, see the Section on Chance in Chapter 5. The possibility of an unexpected random event that is not in your favor is ever present.

As an example of how to apply the idea of the *iterative how's*, consider a hypothetical completed project, viewed as successful with no red flags of which an engineering manager is aware. First he states the success, or the task that is going well: "Our X-C-Lent Product has had no problems in the field since its market introduction twelve months ago." He assumes this is so because of good engineering. Since he is responsible for the company's engineering design for this product, he feels on top of the world. But to fully understand, he asks the first iterative how question: "How has it had no problems in the field?" To answer this question, he plans to begin by asking it of an engineer from quality assurance. The quality engineer answers, "No *problems*, are you kidding?   The supplier of Part X had to replace many parts sent back from the field." He said it was a focus on that part that corrected a number of problems. You now follow this branch of questioning, asking a cognizant development engineer: "How has Part X been improved to make our X-C-Lent Product more reliable?" His answer goes into design and application issues associated with X-C-Lent Product and Part X. The manager can keep going down this branch of *how* questions to whatever level of detail is required. He decided to ask a field service technician, starting down another branch of iterative how's. She answers, "No *problems*, are you kidding? At least one in twenty cannot be installed by the customer without someone from field service walking them through it. The XYZ connection sequence is too complicated." You now can ask, "How did you get the XYZ connection sequence to not be too complicated?" And so on.

Feeling good as the result of things going well is usually based on an incorrect assumption of "how this happened". Looking deeper may turn good feelings into concern by the discovery of red flags.

Ask why, when anything goes poorly

Last night, my wife and I were in an electronics store buying a new mobile phone for her. Things went wrong. It took four hours to cancel her existing account with one carrier, port her current telephone number to her new line, and add her new line to my account with my carrier. Twenty people that were behind us in line when we started were able to buy phones, upgrade contracts, and complete complex transactions, all while we were sitting there struggling with our transaction. We were still there after the store closed—my wife, our salesperson, the cleaning crew, and I. Our salesperson was not the reason; he was knowledgable, extremely helpful, and energetic. We all joked what else could go wrong because everything did every step of the way, starting with a persistent, enigmatic, software error message.

When something is going or has gone poorly, you should search for the root cause; it is a way to understand. Tools for troubleshooting and finding root cause of a problem include one of the better known and simplest: the *five why's* process. Ask yourself, and others, *why* five times, and you will uncover the essence of an issue, the root cause of a problem, or come to see things more clearly. Like a little child that keeps asking *why* to each successive answer, keep asking to zero in on the cause which is not always what it first appears to be. While doing this, any answer must explain the facts and what distinguishes the problem from a similar thing with no problem. For example, say a wheel came off a car while being driven. The questioning could go like this: "Why did the wheel come off? Because all five lug nuts unscrewed." This is observed fact. "Why did all five lug nuts unscrew? Because the design of the threads is wrong." This answer is speculation, not fact. What is more, it does not explain why not one lug nut on the other three wheels are even loose. Distinguishing the problem wheel from the other three with no problem is crucial. It leads to the fact that a flat was repaired one month ago. Another try: "Why did all the lug nuts unscrew? Because they all were not tightened properly when the flat was repaired." This is an assumption and not yet fact. "Why were they not tightened properly? Because..." Now further investigation is required. Assumptions and speculation are alright as long as you use them to guide fact finding, or bridge a gap in data. It may be close to impossible to obtain the truth in certain situations. In this example, how can it be determined that an excellent auto mechanic was distracted and did not install the tire properly? When testing the probable cause, some assumptions may never be turned into fact.

Back to our mobile phone problem of last night. The root cause appears to be that my current mobile phone account is a business account (news to me), discovered at the end of the fourth hour, and a line under a family plan cannot be added to a business account. But this is not the root cause. The root cause is that the software error message that popped up in the first five minutes of our registration process was in a cryptic, unintelligible code. If this error message were in plain language and easier to understand, then the salesperson could have saved four hours on the telephone. By finding the cause and changing the error message, even I as unknowledgeable as I am in these things could provide continuous improvement to the carrier's retail process.

If ever there is a difference between actual results and intended results, ask *why*. More likely than not, you will find the root cause and contributing causes. These will lead to decisions and actions, but as a minimum, you will acquire a better understanding.

JUDGMENT AND DECISION

Understanding is only one part of Overarching Principle #1. Making a decision and taking action complement understanding. One does not always have to take action, but one does have to always make a decision; no action requires a decision not to take action. Understanding is improved during decision-making. Most decisions are made informally in the solitude of one's head, but many times, the decision is made with others in a more formal process.

Decision making is a process. During the time you are arriving at understanding, the objective of the decision and a number of alternatives as potential lines of action will present themselves; and if not, then an objective must be established and a number of alternatives must be creatively generated. The objective has requirements, such as "cannot be more than 8 feet high," or "minimize the weight," and these can be weighted based on importance. Each alternative can be scored as to how well it satisfies each importance-weighted requirement. The alternatives with the highest total weighted score fit the requirements best and should be develop further. In theory, the process works well from an analytical viewpoint, but in practice, it only works with good judgment.

Judgment enters into decision making at the beginning when the objective of the decision is formulated into a statement. The broader the statement, then the larger the scope of the decision, requiring greater effort and more time, but producing a greater effect. For example, before stating the objective "Select and purchase the type and brand of machine for automating the assembly of Parts A, B, and C in production," one broader and more strategic might be stated, "Select the best method of improving the assembly of Parts A, B, and C, including the current method of assembling by hand." Deciding on the scope requires judgment.

Decision at one level of scope or degree of broadness leads to another more specific and less strategic. After the first decision led to automated assembly as being the best method in our example, then the question of type and brand of machine becomes appropriate. When you get down to selecting the features of the machine, or its color, the objectives for the decision become detailed and not strategic. Always start at the broadest, most strategic objective statement that is appropriate for you and the situation. Any statement of the objective for the decision must comply with the higher purpose of the organization.

The statement of the objective for the decision is broken down into a list of requirements. Continuing with the example, for the decision statement "Select and purchase the type and brand of machine for automating the assembly of Parts A, B, and C in production," the list of requirements might be "minimum production rate required is 100 assemblies per hour; the maximum production rate is 500 assemblies per hour; the machine must be able to handle the configuration of the parts and future planned parts; the allowable floor space is 7 ft by 10 ft; the investment should be minimized but no more than $60,000"; and so on. Some requirements are expressed quantitatively and others qualitatively. The characteristics of each alternative are scored as we discussed. All this can be put in a table or matrix format to visualize better.

Judgment still enters into the process of decision making even though what I described is a straight forward analytical exercise. Selecting and wording the requirements and putting numbers on these requirements takes judgment. Why was 500 assemblies per hour picked as the maximum rate needed? Was it because current peak production demand required it, or because it allows for growth in production, and if so, is the added cost of the machine an investment you are willing to propose for an uncertain future benefit? Judgement is also needed in guessing the design and configuration of future planned parts so the machine has the potential to handle them.

Judgment plays a larger role in decisions relating to people. Not only is the selection of the criteria for performance a matter of opinion, but judging whether an individual meets or exceeds any one of the requirements is opinion. I have witnessed where one manager rated a worker as excellent, seeing his value to the organization, while another manager rated the person as poor, seeing little value.

The assessment of an individual is a decision that has all the parts of the decision making process, but relying even more on judgment.

Even though the decision making process can be rational and logical as described above, as it should be, remember that the underlying effectiveness of the outcome is based on judgment. The following is Overarching Principle #2:

Overarching Principle #2:

No decision is effective or useful until sound judgment is applied to an appropriate objective within a higher purpose, and accepted by those who are responsible for implementation.

In summary, understanding first, then deciding, and then acting, as a process, should operate throughout your use of the refined leadership model and all its components and actionable elements. This process occurs continually in your head as you encounter the many situations and interactions daily. You decide whether the importance, urgency, and potential impact are enough to elevate the process to a formal activity for others in which to engage, with or without your involvement. When those who have to implement the decision are involved in the process that arrived at that decision, they will have more commitment in its success.

THE MODEL

"My Intention being to acquire the Habitude of all these Virtues, I judg'd it would be well not to distract my Attention by attempting the whole at once, but to fix it on one of them at a time, and when I should be Master of that, then to proceed to another, and so on till I should have gone thro' the thirteen. And as the previous Acquisition of some might facilitate the Acquisition of certain others, I arrang'd them with that View..."

On his method for self-improvement,
Benjamin Franklin, The Autobiography of Benjamin Franklin[1]

As an engineering department head, I once had a supervisor of design drafting reporting to me, and in turn he had all machine designers reporting to him. He was an ex-marine and ran his group with machine-like efficiently. For a management style, he believed in a military-type chain of command. Oh, did I say he ran his group efficiently? The first time I became involved in the preparation of an engineering drawing, it was completed with the content exactly as I requested of the supervisor. You may ask, "yeah, so, what's wrong with that?" It was exactly, *exactly* as I requested: nothing more, nothing less. When I let him know items were not included, and in general it was not what I had in mind, he said it was exactly what I explained I wanted. Upon reflection, I had to admit he was right; I got what I asked for, literally. I did not realize he was not going to interpret my request and read my intentions. I learned from that point to be more precise in my requests.

It seems like a dream situation for a manager, having an employee who provides exactly what is requested. However, do you know how hard it is to state exactly what one needs done in detail, while trying not to omit anything, with the end result coming from nothing assumed or implied, but only stated explicitly? It is as if one has an efficient and mistake-free automaton working for them.

From the start until when we no longer worked together, the supervisor and I worked as a team in a friendly and professional manner. We laughed when I referred to him as my magic black box. This is when I came up with the idea of the magic black box with respect to work processes.

What if you were to have a magic black box that you could walk up to, state what you want, and out the back pops exactly what you asked for? Work performed in this way involves no people element. With the supervisor of design drafting, this was the situation I experienced, pure analytical efficiency of routine work with no emotion, empathy, or rapport as factors—it was as if I found a specimen in the wild, my Galapagos Islands, isolating a phenomenon in its natural state. This led to the idea for me of the component of JOB in the model of leadership.

With JOB at the center, I built a graphical model that is used to illustrate the complex connections of people aspects in going beyond managing to leadership. The model has components that are representative of going further than just directing and supervising the technical content of an individual's work by a technical manager. As any good model, it makes it easier to see the functioning of the object of study. People leadership is a complex topic, and a graphical model helps as a guide.

WALKING THROUGH THE MODEL

Figure 3.1, *Overview of Refined Leadership Model*, depicts the model. The model is for each individual for whom you are responsible or have an interest in their success. You may have formal authority over the individual represented by the model, or no formal authority, such as with a co-member of a team. The leader as defined here is you. The individual as defined here is each individual with whom you interact. One model is for one individual. If you have five reports, or five on your team, then you will be dealing with five models of leadership, one per individual. Each model for a given individual will be vastly different from the next. You have heard before that you need to manage each person differently. Well, the refined leadership model provides the understanding of why this matters and how to do it.

The model centers around JOB, the outlined rectangle, which is a job function or a position description which involves an analytical-oriented *managing only*. If getting the work done were just a matter of executing to a position description exactly to specification with an efficient and mistake-free automaton, then that would be pure JOB in the model. By the way, you still would have a problem with getting the work performed because you would not be able to communicate accurately and precisely what you would want done, like the magic black box. Continuing from JOB and walking through the model, I will introduce the other *components*.

The people components that intertwine and extend JOB are shown in Figure 3.1. SUBSTANCE is the make-up of that individual, including abilities, skills, talents, background, beliefs, and standards. The personality of the individual is part of his or her SUBSTANCE. The interlacing with JOB is where the capabilities of the individual match the position description and the unwritten requirements of the position. The individual comes with the skills specific for JOB, or they are improved and developed through education and training. The attributes and traits other than capabilities that make up the individual's SUBSTANCE that are relevant are used when needed in performing the work of JOB. As an example, this may be the ability to communicate well, to read the body language of others, and to interpret what others need, but not required to perform pure JOB.

STATURE of an individual is separate from his or her SUBSTANCE and JOB. SUBSTANCE and JOB can influence STATURE, but one could be of much SUBSTANCE, but lack STATURE; or the reverse, they can be of great STATURE in an organization, but lack the high qualities of SUBSTANCE. STATURE is degree of autonomy, freedom of action and expression, importance, ability to get things done, of being heard, and having visibility. Just doing one's JOB, executing the position description, can be done without STATURE; however, the individual would find it impossible to overcome the difficulties and achieve goals associated with change, innovation, and growth without having any degree of STATURE. Overcoming inertia to accomplish something new requires the appropriate amount of STATURE.

MEANING, the next component to be introduced, is provided to the individual by the leader. It deals with why the individual, the leader, or any of the people in the organization, are there doing what they are doing in the first place. MEANING is essential for leadership. The manager leader provides MEANING by establishing a purpose, and framing that purpose by making it personal for the individual. The primary vehicle for providing MEANING, understanding SUBSTANCE, influencing STATURE, and supporting JOB, is the relationship between the manager and the individual.

MEANING, SUBSTANCE, and STATURE are of a different nature than JOB—they are in the province of human nature. These components outside JOB are sensitive to good leadership, and they are pow-

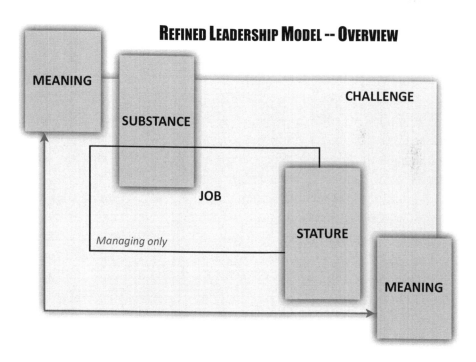

Fig. 3.1 Overview of Refined Leadership Model. Shows the components of the model; model is unique for each individual for whom you are responsible or have an interest in their performance.

erful components in influencing the effectiveness of the individual in the realm of CHALLENGE, the last component of the model.

CHALLENGE is the area outside JOB and *managing only*. Needing more than the knowledge and skills the individual needs for JOB, CHALLENGE encompasses MEANING, SUBSTANCE, and STATURE, as well as JOB. In CHALLENGE, the individual goes beyond the usual tasks, activities, and expectations of JOB, where the individual stretches and grows, and where the organization finds new solutions and is driven for change. All the components of the model need to be present for a given individual, with the leader behind the scenes supporting and encouraging the individual, for success in CHALLENGE.

Why separate leadership into these components? So you can differentiate in order to focus on SUBSTANCE, STATURE, JOB and MEANING. Each component contributes to good leadership. Balancing an individual's SUBSTANCE with his or her STATURE will help the individual better perform his or her JOB, as well as enabling the individual to accomplish CHALLENGE beyond JOB. Influencing all the components of the model for a given individual within the organization for whom you are responsible is your work as leader.

Let us do a thought experiment. Imagine a machine designer reporting to the supervisor from my magic black box story, sitting in a cubicle tediously producing detailed drawings, one after another, looking up reference material on hardware, nuts and bolts, eight hours per day, five days per week, in a vacuum. Let us say the supervisor exhibited none of the methods of refined leadership, but was a no-nonsense, do what I say, just get the drawing done, kind of manager. Now visualize our imaginary machine designer. He is not able to put any of his personal strengths and unique talents into his work; he is not consulted for ideas or heard when he speaks; he is not given any task of much importance or being allowed to feel important. In addition, he is not assigned any work of novelty and has no interaction outside of his immediate surrounding, being informed of only what he needs to know by his supervisor. He is just performing JOB; no other components of the model are a factor.

What consequence to him or the company does the work in the confines of JOB have for our imaginary designer? How can he grow in his profession or as a person? Will he ever feel a sense of accomplishment? Maybe his supervisor will, but I doubt the machine designer will. Will his expectations of himself be forever low? Because of the management style of his supervisor, this designer would not be a factor in the entrepreneurial growth and innovative success of the company. If all the employees were managed this way, I doubt our imaginary company would grow or succeed at all.

THE MODEL'S ACTIONABLE ELEMENTS

Understanding Figure 3.1, *Overview of Refined Leadership Model*, is not enough for you to know how to proceed in implementing the components of the model. These components, JOB, CHALLENGE, SUBSTANCE, STATURE, and MEANING, can be broken down further into *elements* that are on a working level, and that are used to interact with a given individual for whom you are responsible. The leader influences and affects each element of the model, except for maybe the element of *Person*. Influencing Person is dependent on the duration and depth of involvement with an individual.

Figure 3.2, *The Refined Leadership Model*, shows working level elements associated with leadership. MEANING is made up of *Purpose* and *Relationship*. CHALLENGE is composed of *Unexplored*, *Chance*, and *Creativity*, all firmly in the domain of leadership. SUBSTANCE is composed of *Standards*, *Person*, and *Capabilities*. JOB is made up of *Responsibilities*, *Practice*, and *Capacity*, and is the province of managing only. STATURE has as its elements *Autonomy*, *Importance*, and *Power*.

Throughout the course of reading this book and coming to grips with the ideas presented, you should refer back to Figures 3.1 and 3.2. They will help put, and keep, what you read in context for the whole of managing and leading.

Please note: I will explain in more detail the use of each element in the following chapters. Each chapter is dedicated to one component of the model, such as MEANING or SUBSTANCE. But for now, I offer a brief description of each element of Figure 3.2.

Model elements of MEANING

Purpose is the reason you and the individual, for whom a given model represents, are there at work, and why you are in a leadership role. The work being done, and the outcome for which you and the individual are striving, can be identified with a business vision and the higher purpose of the organization. Objectives of the business and immediate goals of the individual are found in Purpose. Your organization's place within a business arena or an industry, as well as the competitive level of its core technologies and the know-how of its people, are included in Purpose.

Relationship is the association and partnership between you, as leader, and the individual. It is the primary vehicle for better communication between you and the individual, and it is dependent on your communication skills. Truthfulness is a large part of Relationship. Rapport and trust cannot be established between you and another without Relationship. Only by Relationship will you know what is important to each individual, their dreams and desires, plans, and personal goals, in addition to his or her unique personality and

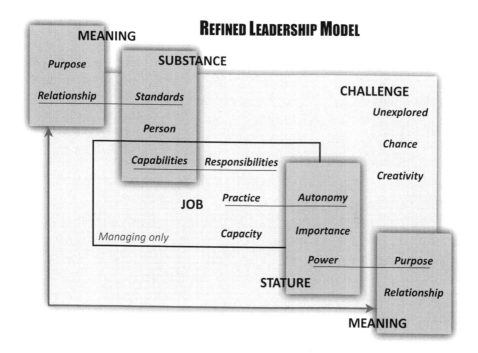

Fig. 3.2   The Refined Leadership Model. Shows elements for each component of the model for which you have an effect upon and are responsible for as leader; model is unique for each individual.

separate, distinct strengths and weaknesses. The element of Relationship is needed to properly engage the technical individual with the business no matter their level in the organization, something rare when managing is devoid of leading. Relationship is essential for the application of Overarching Principle #1, concerning your arrival at full understanding, and for positively influencing an individual in all the elements of the refined leadership model.

Model elements of CHALLENGE

Unexplored is the degree of novelty, and results from a departure from the content of current routine, standard operating procedures, and customary ways. When the individual, or a team, stretches beyond their current responsibilities from their basic position description, they are in the realm of change. Unexplored are new ways of doing, new products, new markets, and new technologies; all which require leaving the comfort of what has been done before and what is done easily everyday with minimal risk and uncertainty.

Chance is the probability of occurrences associated with success and failure. Big factors in success or failure are surprises in outcomes and surprises from random events. The further into change and the more new, and the more distant from standard procedures, the greater the risks, uncertainties, and unknowns, but the greater any potential reward. By embracing and understanding risk and uncertainty, you can increase your opportunity for novelty.

Creativity is the purposeful use of imagination, utilizing different and new perspectives; seeing things differently than before. A large part of leading in this area is group synergy in generating ideas and alternatives for further development. There are no assurances that any ideas of value will emerge, so here also you must embrace the use of random occurrences and surprises. It is here you will focus on helping the individual, and the team, overcome fictitious restrictions from tacit assumptions.

Model elements of SUBSTANCE

Standards are internally existing expectations and acceptable outcomes for the individual, as well as those externally set by the leader and the situation. Standards become the acceptable level of performance and the completeness and quality of the work product. Not only do they define what is expected, they provide consistency across individuals for whom you are responsible. As it turns out, Standards drive performance without pushing or micromanaging from the manager, and for the leader it allows positive and constructive criticism while maintaining a positive atmosphere.

Person is the personality, character, attitude, and beliefs of the individual. Here resides a unique background, professional as well as personal. The individual's cultural heritage, family, and friends make up much of Person. What an individual can attain that could be classified as extraordinary at work is dependent on these areas of uniqueness. Talent, raw abilities that are not work-related, and unusual personal connections with other individuals inside and outside work, all fall under Person.

Capabilities are skills, knowledge, and judgment related to and required for the individual in satisfying the description of the position they occupy, and therefore, the work of JOB. Part of Capabilities comes from the individual's past employment, and part is acquired while with the current organization. Skills and knowledge that are directly needed to succeed at the current position are augmented and reinforced by those unique to the individual and by closely related talents. New skills and knowledge must be added by the individual in order to successfully address change, new products, and new technologies in the realm of CHALLENGE.

Model elements of JOB

Responsibilities are the tasks and functions for which the individual is accountable to the organization. They support the higher values of Purpose and the basic definition of the position description of JOB of which the individual fills. Responsibilities are not those tasks and functions needed in CHALLENGE; instead, the tasks and functions in Responsibilities are associated with those of routine, standard procedures, and standard processes of JOB. Even in an R&D role, where the individual's Responsibilities in JOB are for discovering and developing something new, it is not part of CHALLENGE for that individual. CHALLENGE in R&D is associated with a change in routine, and requires a change in the current rate and current direction of change and innovation—an acceleration of change and innovation.

Practice is the conformance to and the following of standard processes, methodologies, rules, and guidelines. In general, it is how Capabilities and Capacity are carried out. It includes following industry codes and standards, and also conforming to laws and regulations. For learned professionals, it is the customary practice and peer review methodology that arises from collegial professional association.

Capacity is the degree of application of Capabilities and Practice that are possible by the individual. It includes the individual's ability to maintain focus for performing a given quantity of work. Output through persistence with respect to working hard, and effectiveness with respect to working smart, are part of Capacity. Capacity is the ability to do more without sacrificing the expectations and acceptable levels of quality of Standards and Practice.

Model elements of STATURE

Autonomy is the freedom to act through individual initiative, usually independent of the direction from a manager. This is associated with a process of bottom-up decision making and proper delegation. Autonomy is allowing the individual the peace of mind to decide on how they work best, thus obtaining personally optimum work patterns. Autonomy is the freedom to deviate from Practice when appropriate and advantageous to creating something new in the realm of the model component of CHALLENGE. Autonomy is closely allied with the model elements Creativity and Power.

Importance pertains in two ways to the individual: in the significance of the individual's work and in the individual feeling important. As is the case with the other two elements of STATURE, it is the perception by others of the individual and of his or her projects. The climate you create around the individual is a big factor in influencing the element of Importance.

Power is the ability to get things done. It involves a blend of formal and assumed authority. In Power, using strategy and having a tactical vision of seeing a clear direction are crucial abilities in achieving immediate and long term goals. Going through or around obstacles, at times bending, breaking, or ignoring rules and accepted procedures, is much of what Power is about. In addition, success using Power depends on persuasion of others. High visibility of the individual within the organization helps with obtaining and using Power.

More on Components and Elements of the Model

It is important to refer to Figure 3.2, *The Refined Leadership Model*, when you read through the following Chapters in helping you understand the interrelationship of the elements with each other. To maintain the visualization and concept of the components of the model containing the elements, and to keep in mind the bigger picture, refer to Figure 3.1, *The Overview of the Refined Leadership Model*. Remember as you read the following chapters that the leadership model represents a snapshot of the state for one individual at a given time, with the elements filled with content unique to that individual. As the individual grows, the snapshot changes.

SUMMARY OF ACTIONABLE MODEL ELEMENTS

MEANING

Purpose: reason for being there and the work; higher level vision, reason for Relationship, objectives of the business; awareness of place within industry, competitive level of technology and know-how

Relationship: between individual and leader, rapport; primary communication channel; what is important to each, goals; know the other person; establish trust; establish expectations; truthfulness

CHALLENGE

Unexplored: individual and teams stretching from routine of position description, change, new ways, new product development, R&D, new markets, new technologies; associated with risk and uncertainty

Chance: probabilities of success and failure, random negative events, surprises, risks, uncertainties, unknowns; create opportunities for novelty

Creativity: purposeful use of imagination, different and new perspectives, group synergies, using chance occurrences, overcoming fictitious restrictions, generating ideas and alternatives

SUBSTANCE

Standards: internal and external; acceptable level of performance and work product; what's expected, provides consistency, drives performance without pushing, allows for positive and constructive criticism

Person: personality, character, talents, attitude, innate conscientiousness, beliefs; raw technical competencies, unique background; heritage, personal connections, family, friends

Capabilities: skills, knowledge, and judgment required to satisfy the position description; closely related to talents, uniqueness, and internal standards; specifically for JOB, full Substance for CHALLENGE.

SUMMARY OF ACTIONABLE MODEL ELEMENTS
(CONTINUED)

JOB

Responsibilities: tasks and functions for which accountable; part of position description; associated with routine work, may be part of what is used in realm of CHALLENGE

Practice: conformance to or following of standard processes, methodologies, rules, guidelines, and generally how Capabilities and Capacity are carried out in JOB

Capacity: degree of application of Capabilities that are possible by individual; ability to maintain focus, to dig deep, and cover breadth; individual capacities are additive for group or team

STATURE

Autonomy: freedom to act outside Practice, bottom-up decision making, proper delegation, individual initiative; allows personally optimized work patterns

Importance: significance of the individual's work; individual feeling important; perception of others of the individual's importance

Power: the ability to get things done; tactics, strategy, vision of seeing direction; formal and informal authority; persuasion of others; visibility within organization; closely related to Autonomy and Importance

---

Although the model represents one individual, a composite of many models is used for managing and leading a department or group of individuals, or for members of cross-functional teams. You will see how this works as you proceed through each remaining chapter.

The model of leadership is useful in other ways. The model helps in providing areas to focus on when interviewing people for employment. The model gives good guidance on how to select candidates for positions transferring within the company, and how to select team members for projects. In putting together plans for professional development for individuals, the model is a good outline. You can use it as a model representing yourself to better understand your value to the organization, give you direction for self-improvement, and help you visualize areas for personal success. I am sure the model approach to understanding managing and leadership will trigger many good ideas for you to use.

You probably noticed by now that the word for each component of the model is in all capitals, such as STATURE, so you can easily distinguish them, and each element is in the same font as the body of the text, but with a capitalize first letter, such as Autonomy. This scheme is maintained throughout the book.

CRITICAL INTERFACES

Still referring to Figure 3.2, *The Refined Leadership Model*, each underlined pair is a *critical interface* between the the model's components (JOB, SUBSTANCE, STATURE, and MEANING). These critical interfaces connect the components of JOB with SUBSTANCE and STATURE, and SUBSTANCE and STATURE with MEANING. CHALLENGE encompasses all the components and elements of the model, but if an interface were to be identified as existing, then it would be Relationship of MEANING equally connected with Unexplored, Chance, and Creativity. These interfaces are used to navigate the subtleties and intricacies of implementing leadership.

The model elements that make up a critical interface pair help define each other. They are opposing ideas and they must co-exist. Together they balance and oppose; they are countervailing. In addition, it is at each critical interface that much of the traditional management control methods are employed, such as using a formal schedule or a stage and gate process at the interface of Practice and Autonomy, or an ethics policy at the interface of Power and Purpose. The critical interfaces are listed below:

- Relationship-Standards Interface
- Capabilities-Responsibilities Interface
- Practice-Autonomy Interface
- Power-Purpose Interface

Each critical interface has its own sub-chapter later in the book. I present a list of guidelines for each to show how the two elements define, balance, and oppose each other, as well as how they can be used in the organizational setting.

BRIEF EXAMPLE ON THE USE OF THE MODEL

Say you are the manager of a design engineer, who normally executes sales orders by reconfiguring the company's standard packaging machines specifically for customers. She has been assigned by you to lead a team to develop a new, high speed, packaging machine which would be a breakthrough for the industry. Upper management has staked the success of the company on this project.

She has been in her position for a good number of years, being specifically skilled and knowledgeable, with good judgment, in the model component of JOB, executing sales orders. With the three elements of SUBSTANCE, it has been determined she has the potential to go beyond JOB, leading the team for developing this breakthrough product in the area of CHALLENGE. As for the leadership elements of Standards, Person, Capabilities, Responsibilities, Practice, and Capacity, she nicely exceeds the levels you feel are minimum in each for this assignment as became evident over time through JOB.

This is her first product development project. Acting in your leadership role, you have influenced and built her standing in the element of Importance, that is, the importance of the project with her and with the organization and her ability to achieve success leading that project. She knows you support her and that you have confidence in her abilities, and by this you have instilled in her an ever increasing level of self-confidence. You have built her level of STATURE within the organization to be consistence with that of SUBSTANCE and JOB, levels of which she has displayed to you in the past.

Going outside of JOB into CHALLENGE, what about the elements of Purpose, Relationship, Standards, Capabilities, Responsibilities, Practice, Autonomy, and Power? You will have to do some work as her manager, and in a leadership role, in these elements. Since she will be new to leading a project such as this, you will focus on helping her dig deep when necessary to find talents and desire that up to now she did not need to use in JOB. Through the component of MEANING with its elements of Purpose and Relationship, you help find her new objectives in areas that are unfamiliar and uncertain. You will address with the design engineer, and her team (made up of other individuals) at the right time, what you know to be vital as factors of success. What new capabilities do they need? What are their new responsibilities? How independent and self-directed would the cross-functional team be? What portion of time would each member on the team ultimately work on the project, or would they be dedicated full time? To what lengths could they go to get results by bending the rules or taking shortcuts with company standard procedures and policies? To what degree over budget and behind schedule could be tolerated? How acceptable would it be for her to use outside services and consultants, or how easily would it be to get others to agree to reallocate resources from other parts of the company? What would be the limits of her team's decision making? You must ask yourself, could a partiality with the design engineer cloud your objectivity with judging performance and results, and are you giving too little or too much freedom and power? The answers to these questions are trade-offs that must be weighed and balanced and are found in the four critical interfaces of leadership.

The Relationship-Standards Interface sets the standards in general for JOB, but specifically for special situations in CHALLENGE. The rapport and communication between you and the design engineer has to be on-going throughout the project. At first you help set guidelines and rules of engagement with her and her team; then as the project progresses and as issues arise, you have dialogue with all involved to interpret Standards. This interface keeps you from relaxing expectations, not holding her accountable, or letting favoritism influence judgment; but, it also keeps you closely in support.

Continuing with our example, the Capabilities-Responsibilities Interface finds from the universe of the design engineer's overall abilities what is needed to succeed at her position in the organization at JOB, but now even more so for what is needed for her new project. As you discovered, Capabilities she used for JOB are much less than the broader skills, knowledge, and judgment she brought from training, education, and experience from previous positions, schooling, and life experiences. You did not define her potential by a perception based on the little you once knew of her abilities. For the project in CHALLENGE, you must help her and her team apply available Capabilities to their identified new objectives.

The Practice-Autonomy Interface balances to what degree there exists a freedom from the routine, customary procedures, and formal processes normally accepted as part of the design engineer's work. The independence she is encouraged to have by you, or takes upon herself, will affect the other elements of STATURE, that is, Importance and Power. The kind and amount of independence with which the design engineer is comfortable, and you should offer and encourage, is dependent on how much of Practice is demanded by the various situations that arise with the project. It takes good judgment in not being constrained by standard practice, company procedures, and industry codes and standards when creating something new, and yet in not creating the possibility that the work will result in anything unsafe or grossly misguided.

The Power-Purpose Interface sets appropriate, yet flexible, boundaries of action. The extent she and the team can go to get things done, or to address an opportunity, is limited based on the appropriateness with Purpose, goals and objectives. She and her team cannot rob a bank to acquire funds for the project. This would be out of balance as a trade-off, and not consistent with the business purpose of the project, not to mention its illegality. But they can redirect the budget for an activity within the project to another activity within the same project to address a technical and business opportunity. It hurts no one and it favorably supports project objectives. The understanding and existence of Purpose for the design engineer and her team is the leader's responsibility and is closely related to Relationship, both elements of MEANING, the subject of our next chapter.

CHAPTER 4

PROVISION FOR MEANING

"Give me that which I want, and you shall have this which you want, is the meaning of every such offer; and it is in this manner that we obtain from one another the far greater part of those good offices which we stand in need of. It is not from the benevolence of the butcher, the brewer, or the baker that we expect our dinner, but from their regard to their own interest. We address ourselves, not to their humanity but to their self-love, and never talk to them of our own necessities but of their advantages."

Adam Smith, The Wealth of Nations[1]

An engineer would be fortunate if once in their career they experienced an exceptional work environment of purpose and creation. From the factories of manufactured products to the construction sites of buildings, from the design offices of infrastructure projects to the operating plants of utilities, and from the corporate corner office to the government agency, creating for a higher purpose is the heart of the engineering profession. Young men and women go into engineering in the first place for this reason, to satisfy the needs of society. They see themselves making living easier for many by solving the problems of living day to day, and making life possible by solving the problems of the world.

I was fortunate to experience such an environment in a small private company that was growing rapidly and profitably. From the board of directors on down, there existed a purpose for which all functional departments were aligned. By no means was the company perfect, but for anyone who wanted to develop important products and take them to market, it was a special place to work. However, purpose alone was not sufficient to bring about the magical chemistry within that company without the personal expression of that purpose in terms that meant something to each worker.

For any enterprise or endeavor, or for any change you want to make, you will need two essentials: 1) have a purpose, and 2) establish relationships toward that purpose. Leadership cannot be simplified further. Everything in business and industry will flow from this origin. In terms of the refined leadership model, these two essentials make up MEANING.

ELEMENTS OF MEANING

- Purpose
- Relationship

MEANING derives from the refined leadership elements of Purpose and Relationship. Defining and interpreting aim and aspiration in the context of work for an individual transforms labor into passion; and transforms you in their eyes from someone more than just a person assigning them to their tasks. Developing a personal connection with an individual for whom you are responsible, or for whom you have a stake in the their success, is the way to reach beyond being a supervisor, or a manager, to being someone who allows them to see their place in it all.

Purpose can be categorized by end benefit first and by scope of task second. The goodness of the end benefit and the strategic level of the goal determine the degree of higher purpose. The more noble the ends, such as one that provides safety or one that provides health care, and the more strategic the objective, such as creating a new product platform or new service for the company to provide the end benefit, then the higher the purpose. Higher purpose has nothing to do with not being in it for profit; making a profit is good for everyone. An individual earning a living for his or her family by performing lower level tasks, and helping a company make a profit, can be of the highest purpose for that individual and society.

A connection at work that you establish with each individual for whom you are responsible is unique. Your continual interaction with the individual occurs through the leadership element Relationship, and along with the conveyance of Purpose, directly influences initiative and performance of that individual, and better outcomes for the organization.

WITH NO PURPOSE, THERE IS NO RELATIONSHIP

You as leader and the individual have a reason for being together each day and expending great effort. The obvious reason for each of you, and most practical, is to make a living, to pay the bills. Where you work is determined by practical factors, such as geographic location and job availability. Only a lucky few wind up doing exactly what they would have chosen to do in this world. Nevertheless, you are being payed by someone to perform in some way, therefore, you and the individual are there not just for the good reason of survival, but for the good reason of working toward a purpose related to why you are being compensated. It is an exchange of value that is at the heart of what makes work noble, a providing for oneself in a free society and in turn benefiting that society.

With work as an exchange of value, you provide your services and your employer pays you for those services. As soon as one side of that arrangement is not obtaining equal value from the other side, the arrangement is at risk of being changed; either the worker leaves the company or organization, or the worker is terminated. This exchange of value is directly related to how the company creates value. There is much written on adding value in an enterprise. I will not go into it here, except to say the reality you help create for the individual is tied closely to the value creation of the company.

As leader, you translate the many needs and objectives of the organization into a basis for motivation for the individual. Most professionals are driven by this; I know engineers are internally driven, self-motivated, more by working toward a higher purpose than by money alone. Do an experiment someday. Ask twenty engineers why they are in engineering. I bet a large majority, if not all, do not answer because they want to become wealthy. It is the same for teachers, nurses, and other professionals who see their profession as a calling. The third overarching principle is as follows:

Overarching Principle #3:

A connection made, and maintained, between the technical and the business sides of the organization attaches value to the work of a technical professional.

You as leader build a relationship based on shared purpose, a purpose that is mutual or common between you both. If you were not to have a shared purpose with the individual for whom you are responsible, then you are at risk of requiring a style of leadership more toward command-and-control than refined leadership. You would try to force the individual to dance to a tune that you only hear; you would have to instruct them every step of the way for them to do their work. Allowing the individual to share aspirations with you as leader is much more rewarding, and fun, for you and the individual.

Your work as a technical leader is to understand both domains affecting the success of the organization, that of the technical side and that of the business side. You are at a unique position situated at the nexus of the technical talent of the company and internal and external customers requiring its use. You are there to examine and convert business needs into viable propositions, action plans, and usable results, based on the business side's guidance for those needs. You as leader have to make the connection and may have to translate for others. You will need to straddle the gulf between both worlds, effectively communicating in terms to which others are accustomed.

Sharing a purpose with another is made easier by your relationship, and your relationship is made easier by sharing a purpose. Purpose gives the reason for the relationship.

ELEMENT: PURPOSE

I once reported to a CEO who was convinced that engineers, designers, and technicians would meet their technical obligations better by knowing next quarters financial targets, such as EBITDA or sales projections by product line and sales region, or by knowing by heart the performance results on charts on a wall of another functional department. He would stop to quiz engineering personnel on the finer points of what in essence were the immediate working goals and performance metrics of others, and if he or she answered incorrectly, I would hear afterward how it was no wonder so and so cannot get a particular technical task completed on time. The CEO failed to understand they had immediate working goals of their own that had to be meaningful for them on a working level in their current, and difficult, projects. Arcane financial detail and the specific performance metrics of others are not useful to those who had to focus elsewhere. Knowing whether or not manufacturing met last months production targets, and by how much, did not help the personnel who were absorbed in unrelated matters of fine detail required of design, prototyping, testing, and fabrication, literally ranging from nuts and bolts up through the laws of science and engineering. On any particular day, development engineers, designers, and technicians were trying to solve many theoretical and practical technical puzzles related to the functioning of complex machines. Under time pressure, issues relating to industry standards, quality, safety, manufacturability, parts suppliers, competitive technology, as well as hundreds of project details, consumed their thinking and action each day. An immediate purpose translated from a higher purpose is what drove their action.

Same higher purpose, different immediate goals

Everyone in a company or organization should be working for the same higher purpose and strategic objectives. On a working level, individuals cannot achieve these higher objectives, but they can achieve supporting, tactical objectives. The element Purpose of the refined leadership model keeps higher purpose in the forefront by stating objectives in terms relevant and consequential for the individual. Higher purpose must be understood as the intended end results of the individual's work, but in terms that mean something to the particular focus and reality of that worker, even if others in the organization have different, but complementary, focus and reality.

In any organization, work needs to be performed at many levels with lower level activities being consistent with business plans. Any given intended end result will fall within a range from the most strategic to least strategic, from CEO to individual contributor; or viewing it in the obverse, ranging from the least tactical to most tactical. Being more tactical requires more attention and deeper focus for specific, immediate, working goals. The content of this depth and detail (e.g., spending weeks selecting a suitable material of construction for a fabricated part), and not the CEO's broad view (e.g., in minutes answering a question on the materials policy for the company's products), is the individual contributor's immediate reality.

Purpose governs degree of intimacy

The reason for the work association affects the appropriate depth of a particular relationship with an individual, as well as the proper amount of time and effort in developing that relationship. It is Purpose that determines how much you should come to know of the individual, and they should come to know of you.

The relationship between two people discussed in connection with refined leadership is not intended to be for friendship. However, closeness and bonding will result as more is learned by each about the other. The leader can control the degree of intimacy by controlling the nature of the interactions based on the reasons for them. The relationship should be centered around the business purpose you established that brings meaning to the work situation. If the intention of any aspect of a relationship were not to add meaning for the individual or provide better understanding for you or the individual, then reconsider how you are proceeding.

The kind of personal association for a given individual can be defined and expressed based on the strategic level of their responsibilities. Increasingly higher levels of responsibility require increasingly deeper relationships, and increasingly more time and effort. For example, your relationship with a key individual in your group, say a supervisor who reports to you, would be deeper than compared to one with a person who is an individual contributor outside your group with whom you occasionally interact. Your relationship with the supervisor involves interaction every day that directly affects many others in your department and how they support the needs of the organization. Your time together will add to knowing more of the other, and may involve regular lunches and an occasional dinner with spouses. On the other hand, a relationship of this kind and at this level of involvement would be inappropriate, or an ineffective use of your time and energy, for the individual contributor outside your group.

ELEMENT: RELATIONSHIP

Refined leadership is dependent on an association at a working level, interacting day-to-day to positively influence individuals. It could be described as personal to the extent that it is between two people at any one time. This makes Relationship the vehicle for understanding and for influencing all the elements of the refined leadership model.

A personal connection related to work is necessary to learn and to know the individual, revealing the internal standards of the individual, the areas of uniqueness of the person, and the capabilities for his or her work. In addition to knowing the individual, a working association forms the basis for your influence to help the individual find and attain the appropriate independence, be assigned new projects of the highest import, to gain and retain confidence in themselves, and to be able to exert the right kind and degree of power. This brings us to the next overarching principle, and my favorite:

Overarching Principle #4:

Leadership is a unique relationship between two people, repeated as many times as necessary. The leader is responsible to make this relationship positive and meaningful, no matter the difficulties.

The relationship I am describing here is not a friendship. It could develop over a long period of time into a friendship, but for the reasons the leader and the individual come together, or are thrown together, it is not intended for them to be friends. A friendship does not need a purpose to develop and exist between two people, but a professional relationship does. A friendship should not have a purpose for being—our times with good friends should be enough proof of that fact. However, a relationship between the leader and an individual *must* have a purpose, otherwise there is no reason for the relationship. In addition, a friendship does not have to be constrained by standards, but a professional relationship *must* be balanced and constrained by standards.

Some may think personal connections are difficult. In a business setting, it is easy to establish a meaningful relationship by basing it on what needs to be done, focusing the association on the fully understood needs of the business or organization. What is more, the relationship you have with the individual is the primary vehicle for addressing every element of the refined leadership model, giving you ample nuclei around which to concentrate. Also, the element of Relationship operates to link all the elements of leadership: Purpose, Standards, Person, Capabilities, Responsibilities, Practice, Capacity, Autonomy, Importance, Power, Unexplored, Chance and Creativity. As you use each element in the model, you will see how deeply Relationship affects managing and leading the individual.

State of mind directs mental energy

I once worked for a Director of Operations when I was Manager of Engineering for an equipment company. We were working in engineering on developing a new product platform. We worked part time on it with limited resources when we were not working on our immediate responsibilities of executing custom sales orders for the ongoing business. The product was a large, walk-in, fabricated steel affair, so it took some effort to build and modify. We continually had been learning of technical weaknesses in the design from our first prototype, especially the pesky drive mechanism involving a constant velocity joint. We were at the point where we needed some creative solutions to a number of related thorny technical problems. It was then my boss demanded that I have the problem solved, the solution fabricated, and the prototype running by Friday, three days away, when visitors were to be there. His words, "You *will* have this up and running by Friday!" From his tone and facial expression you could read "or else!" Then his body language was dismissive, as if with the house servant just given orders for the day to complete a task that has been performed hundreds of times before, but missed yesterday. He did not ask about details, or explore with me what we knew, or how we might proceed. He did not acknowledge any small aspect of what is presented here as CHALLENGE, or provide Importance, in any way. He did not offer help, he just said do it or else.

He increased my stress, but now with anger thrown in. I suppose he thought by creating more pressure and making threats, we would be more creative. I can assure you, one cannot force creativity by demanding it, or by breeding disabling, negative emotions. The human brain does not work that way.

You will have many opportunities through Relationship to influence an individual in feeling good about himself or herself and having self-confidence. Positive emotions are needed for creative output and for results from the higher functioning of the human brain. Fear and mistrust displace analysis, imagination, logic, and the desire for collaboration.

You should be mindful that putting one you influence in the right frame of mind is the starting point for you in helping that person confront a difficult task or assignment. Why dispirit and deflate an individual with indifference, or worse with confrontation that saps their motivation? Why burden anyone with unnecessary negative thoughts and feelings that just become major distractions?

I have seen managers demand creative technical output while disparaging those of whom they were making the demands, and I have been on the receiving end of similar situations at times. To my way of thinking, the primary function of a manager, and especially of a leader, is to help an individual feel capable and equal to a task. Part of this is to instill a sense of importance by showing them the impact of that task on the overall success of the organization. But as a minimum, a manager, or leader, must allow them to feel important and have confidence in themselves. Poor managers do not even allow this; to them, their own feelings of importance matter more.

Through the leadership model elements of Relationship and Purpose, you make project and company objectives personal and significant for a worker. Through Relationship, you should strive to create an uniquely energizing spirit in and around any task for the individual. In this way, you will provide MEANING, and the benefits of the next overarching principle:

Overarching Principle #5:

A positive emotional state promotes creativity, expressiveness, commitment, and an absorption into work.

Creativity, and other outcomes requiring the higher levels of thinking and emotions, will be covered further in the next chapter, but being so closely related to providing MEANING, I thought it best to introduce Overarching Principle #5 here. I will cover more on positive emotions as they pertain to the model element of Importance in the chapter on STATURE. I mention these ideas here to show how your working relationship with the individual is the way to understand the individual's SUBSTANCE and JOB, and so to be in a position to influence their STATURE. Your close and positive professional association with the individual is the means to those ends.

Establishing Relationships and Your Personality

You do not have to change your personality in order to build relationships. However, you are required to consciously focus more attention on your interactions with that individual, concentrating on each of the elements of the model of refined leadership. You need to be aware of the emotional effect your interactions have on that individual. Make a point to learn from every interaction with others; what was the response vs. what you said or did. You may need to improve your skills in reading between the lines, facial expressions, and body language, but if you are intentionally looking for the response, you will be more attuned to those that are non-verbal.

An example just happened to me of how one could learn about interacting with people from everyday encounters, especially from the response of others. One evening, I was with my wife in a store looking for a small gift. As we were leaving, a pleasant young saleswoman asked if we found what we were looking for and my wife said she found some ideas and would be back. I said jokingly with a big smile, "now if you were a good salesperson, you would not let us walk out the door without selling it to us." She became serious with a forced smile and said, "thank you *very* much, sir. I needed *that*, thank you *very* much." I realized I offended her and assured her I was just joking. I tried to be pleasant and it backfired.

After we left the store, I gave some thought to what I said; it became obvious what went wrong. I should have said, "being the exceptional salesperson you *are*, you would not let us walk out the door without selling it to us."   A subtle difference between what I said and what I could have said, but a clear difference in the effect. What I said produced a big negative effect. What I did not say, but could have, I am sure would have elicited a more favorable response, with the salesperson feeling better about herself—and me not feeling like what I appeared to be, an obnoxious person.

You can never know for certain the effect you have on an individual who has responsibilities to perform in a work capacity by the emotions you instill or provoke with your manner of interacting. Most of the time it is not perceptible to you. Unlike the salesperson, they may keep emotions from you, inadvertently or consciously. Remember engineers and other technical professionals are knowledge workers, most of their creative contribution to the business begins, and may even end, in their heads. Around the clock in any location, thinking continues, unseen and unknown to anybody until they choose to act on that thinking. How they feel at any given time directly affects the individual's thinking and indirectly their actions. As leader, this is where you have an invisible, but drastic effect.

It should have become apparent by now that being good at communicating is an important tool in building relationships and leading others. The remainder of this section will present some pointers to help build those skills.

Manner of Interacting

I strongly recommend that you never instill fear or create an atmosphere of uncertainty by what you say or do. In fact, what you say and do should help overcome fear and uncertainty for whom you are responsible. I tried my hand at sales for a short time in my career as a sales engineer selling capital equipment and manufacturing systems for polymer compounding. I had a boss who, in addition to being a true gentleman and a refined leader, was an excellent salesman. During one sales call he accompanied me on, the engineer in me came out. I tried to help the prospective customer get all his facts and details correct. It was a competitive situation and we were not the preferred supplier. Afterward, he instructed me that in this sales situation my approach was not the best.

He said, "you should have used fud."

Not sure I heard him right, I asked, "fud?"

"Yes, F-U-D, FUD" first saying each letter separately with emphasis. He continued, "you should instill *fear, uncertainty*, and *doubt* when you do not want the sales prospect to make a decision when a competitor is favored. Do not make him comfortable with making a decision and acting; paralyze him with fear and uncertainty, make him doubt himself."

Great tactic for a salesperson, but this is just the opposite of what you want to do as a leader, influencing individuals through your dialogue with them to *dispel* fear, uncertainty, and doubt, so they can use the higher functions of the brain for creativity, decision making, and effective action. Interactions drive emotions and positive emotions are required for good and plentiful outcomes from thinking individually or in groups.

As I assured you, it is not necessary for you to change your personality to practice a refined leadership or to establish an appropriate relationship. Your personality only comes into play by how you interact with that individual and what you can read in their facial expressions, their body language, and their message that must be read between the lines. Independent of personality, you can consciously control how you interact and communicate with individuals, making a point to be aware how the other individual has a mental state that affects work performance. This mental state is only observable by you through what the individual says and does, or how they say and do it. Only the inflection of the saleswoman's voice gave me the clue I said the wrong thing. The ability to do this is made easier by knowing the individual better through a work connection and relationship. For some, the ability to read others, even strangers they are meeting for the first time, comes easily; this falls in the area of social intelligence. I was not sure I offended the saleswoman, but if she was not a stranger to me, I would have been sure—and possibly would have known the root cause of her reacting the way she did to my comment. As long as you have the ability to be consistent in the actions and communication that provide positive experiences for the individual for whom you are responsible, then no personality will be an obstacle to refined leadership.

Establishing a relationship and communicating with an individual are easier when tied to Purpose. Unlike trying to make small talk at a cocktail party, discussions with common objectives offer something on which you can focus. Start from where the other person is on the subject with respect to awareness, knowledge, and opinion. Then by dialogue, both can work toward a better understanding of the situation by sharing awareness, knowledge, and opinion.

Good two-way communication is your responsibility as a leader, and not the individual's responsibility. One of the times you should be inflexible and in control is when making sure the conditions are right for meaningful exchange of information, ideas, and points of view. The leader has the formal and moral authority to set the agenda, to say when, where, and how meetings are held for good communication. Also, only you can control your focus on the other person speaking and your caring to hear what is being said.

You and the individual are both obligated to speak openly together when in private, but when in public, you both separately must stand behind and execute the decisions to which you mutually agreed. You must encourage dissension and debate in private in order to discover the true facts and objective evidence, and to arrive at the best ideas for action. However, you must provide and demand of the individual mutual support in public for what was agreed upon in private. This practice is most important at the team level when more than two individuals from different functional departments meet to make decisions and then go their separate ways to execute the decisions. It will help combat the creation of a culture that is petty in the form of gossip and that is destructive in the form of self-serving criticism of others.

You will make mistakes and you will misspeak at times; it is how you correct those mistakes and what you learn from them that makes all the difference. Stay relaxed when admitting a slip of the tongue or a blunder in a point you are trying to make. The important thing is to apologize when you offend the other person, but the result of the majority of your communication mistakes will be only your personal embarrassment, and those who may be embarrassed for you.

CONNECTING AND LISTENING THROUGH RAPPORT

The path to understanding, to establishing a positive and meaningful relationship on a working level, and to translating higher purpose to immediate purpose and goals is you being an exceptional listener. It is the important part of two-way communication. This is also the path to learning the SUBSTANCE of an individual, supporting that person in his or her JOB and in CHALLENGE, and influencing his or her STATURE. In general, better communication occurs when both parties listen better, especially when a connection is made through rapport.

Rapport is a mutual and harmonious connection made between two people and results in each easily understanding the ideas of the other. Rapport enhances empathy, allowing one person to feel what the other feels. When in a state of rapport, interactions are pleasant and smooth. In this state, two or more individuals have a higher probability of collaboratively being more creative and of making good decisions. We have all experienced such meeting of the minds, where one could almost finish the sentence for the other person and ideas from one build upon ideas of the other in a synergistic and flowing manner. Body language, facial expressions, and listening mechanics are a big part of the connection. As a leader, the ability to set the conditions for establishing rapport between you and an individual for whom you are responsible is a powerful tool.

Recognizing rapport as an observer during a given interaction between two other people is important for a leader of engineering personnel; it tells you plenty of the chemistry between the individuals and adds to your understanding of them. Just as with you and another person, setting the conditions for rapport between others establishes a collegial environment.

You know how with some people you feel comfortable, but with others you *can never connect*? Making a connection with another person is easier when coming from a similar background, and when alike in many ways. It is infinitely easier for one trial lawyer from New York to communicate with another trial lawyer from New York than for a trial lawyer from New York to communicate with a research chemist from Minneapolis. The task for you as leader is to overcome any dissimilarities you may share in order to establish rapport, finding a way to connect when it is necessary to do so.

As leader, good communication with those you lead is *your* responsibility. Therefore, you need to be certain that the right conditions are present to encourage the occurrence of rapport. One of the most important requirements for you is to pay attention to the other person. When the other person sees that you are focusing on him or her, listening intently, he or she senses you care. This requires you to put down what you are doing, turn away from the computer, do not answer the phone, and forget any ideas of multitasking. Do not be preoccupied and do not daydream or let your mind stray. Giving total attention for the purpose of listening has a secondary benefit to that of fostering rapport, and that is, you listen better. Listening gives you the ability to gain full understanding of a situation or circumstances as is needed in the practice of a refined leadership.

Besides focusing and intently listening, another important condition in promoting rapport is to achieve and maintain an atmosphere of good feeling. If you or the other person were angry, were experiencing fear, or were emotionally stressed, rapport would be unlikely and good communication would not be possible. If mistrust or a dislike were to exist with you or the other person, or with you both, any communication would not be of the kind that results from a rapport. Therefore, keep emotions positive.

Another interesting condition that may either be the result of rapport, or the cause, I am not sure which, is the phenomenon of synchrony. When we speak and listen, we show body language. Sometimes one's body language says more than the words one speaks. Synchrony is a simultaneous matching of body language while communicating: facial expressions, position while sitting or standing, and body motions. One can become uneasy during a conversation when *out of sync* with the other person. Have you ever spoken with someone who never smiled or nodded in response, or kept looking past your head at something behind you? It is quite unnerving. So the lesson is to show the other person you are listening, and that you sincerely care about them; but above all, let your body language communicate this by letting synchrony occur naturally.

Finally, do not run down an agenda of points you want to make, if you want to establish a rapport. When promoting the occurrence of rapport, you must resist the tendency to interrupt the other person with what you want to say. Let the other person make his or her points. Not only will you promote rapport by not interrupting, but you may learn even more by listening in this manner.

Establishing rapport and listening intently not only requires your focus, but it requires your time. Having many individuals as direct reports, demands on your time will be high. This may be part of the problem with engineers making the transition to management and leading: they may not want to spend so much time on people issues at the expense of engineering work. To lead properly, your involvement with people will be increasingly more important than the technical tasks to which you personally give attention.

RELATIONSHIP BALANCED BY STANDARDS

The interface between relationship and standards keeps in check any potential adverse business affects resulting from a relationship that becomes too close or inappropriate. Standards here refer to three ideas: 1) the standards that are internal to the individual with which you have a relationship; 2) the standards imposed by the manager consistent for all individuals within a group or profession; and 3) the standards you impose on your conduct pertinent to the relationship. To keep the relationship appropriate and work related, the second and third points above are critical.

Reprimands do not have to become personal or negative. Holding individuals to high expectations of work quality and results is accomplished through the standards you set consistent for the group and for a class of activities. As an example, let us assume that you require of each engineer a weekly report, due on Friday morning, on which you rely to prepare your weekly report for your boss, due Friday afternoon. On this one occasion, now Friday at 2:00 PM, an engineer has not submitted his report. You could leave a blistering voicemail, flexing your authority. Instead, you decide to find the individual to see what happened. This way, you will understand more, you will not create negative emotions, and you will reinforce the standard that concerns reporting. You find the engineer hard at work at an urgent task away from his desk in the manufacturing area. Now you know the reason for the missed report. You need to keep the engineer energized and his emotions high, but you also need to reprimand his delinquency with the report despite the important task he was doing. You ask, "Bill, how's it going?"

Bill, pointing to a complex assembly on a production unit: "Not so good, this interferes with the pressure control sensor, but we found a solution." Picking up a bracket, "We think this will fix it."

You say, "I see what your saying. Looks good. I know this is important right now, but have you forgotten the status report?"

Bill, just slightly defensive: "No, but I was doing this since yesterday afternoon. Why do we have to do that anyway? It is just a waste of time!" You reinforce why this standard exists for the group.

Finding a solution suitable for now and for the long term, you say something like this, "For now, give me a quick verbal report and I will use that for today. Later, you and I will see what we can come up with so the report won't take up much time or be late in the future."

He was in a difficult position and you were making sure both obligations were met. You kept the situation positive, since you both were striving to do the right thing. Making it personally difficult through criticism and harsh words does not keep the individual producing at a high level. Using Standards set by internal and external expectations of the individual, you enforce what needs to be done without adversely affecting the relationship needed for the continued practice of refined leadership with that individual.

A personal connection cannot interfere with performance. The Relationship-Standards Interface of the leadership model guards against chumminess issues or allowing an individual not to pull their own weight. There must not be a double standard by not holding every individual accountable.

Standards are like friction, and having no standards is like trying to walk on ice without traction from friction; you cannot walk fast or be sure of yourself. This is a good type of friction; your association as a leader with an individual gets traction from the element Standards. There is a bad type of friction that results from disagreement and incompatibility. This is like the friction between the moving parts of a machine where a portion of useful energy is turned into waste heat. Relationships may not function efficiently with the bad type of friction around, but it will function more effectively with the good type, assuring traction toward Purpose. Although friction is not good in many areas, the world would be a difficult place in which to live without friction.

TRUTHFULNESS AND ACCOUNTABILITY

I cannot stress enough the detrimental impact of actions by you as a leader that could call into question your sincerity toward those individuals for whom you are responsible. An individual must be assured that he or she can count on your support in times of difficulty or when they face adversity, and that you will represent them with honesty and integrity. I have seen managers who were in the position to be leaders turn out to be despicable in their actions, benefitting themselves at the expense of those for whom they were responsible. It is too easy for a manager to bend the truth about people, and too convenient for a manager to criticize, and find a scapegoat in, an individual.

I can think of more than a few examples of managers in my past who exhibited low character by their actions toward individuals for whom they should have been a supporter and a helper, but instead they were an accuser and an adversary behind their backs. One prominent example that stands out for me is that of a general manager to whom I once reported. Before his promotion to general manager, he and I were peers; he was head of sales and I was head of engineering. It was at this time I noticed his mode of operation. He would find an individual in his group—a product manager, a regional manager, a project manager—to use as a scapegoat to deflect attention from a difficulty he would be having in explaining poor performance in an area for which he was responsible. After a space of time reduced the usefulness of this ploy against the selected individual, he would fire that individual, and turn his sights on another. At the general manager level, he continued this practice, and he ultimately found me a convenient target for his continued survival. His case against me was thin, almost trivial in nature, and I could not agree on the seriousness of the trumped up points. Any one of those points could have been addressed by me easily, especially with his support. But instead, he built a case behind my back to fire me. He needed another red herring to get those to whom he reported off the scent of another deficiency in performance in his area of responsibility. Someone caught on to his game; he was fired three months after he succeeded in firing me.

If this general manager thought that his actions constituted leadership, then it is not the leadership I am promoting. He had individuals reporting to him with much experience in the industry, and those individuals knew the technical and business sides as no others in that industry. He came from outside the industry and tried to cover-up his lack of technical knowledge instead of leading them as a team to higher competitive achievement. The industry was mature and ripe for entrepreneurial change, so it would not have taken much innovation to make a competitive difference. To this day, he stands out for me as a remarkable example of one who was in a position to lead good technical professionals, but who either did not care to, or did not know how to.

Holding yourself accountable for what you have assigned to an individual by considering his or her failure your failure is the only posture a true leader can adopt. A manager responsible for performance in his or her area is the only one in a consistent position of being in contact with what is going on from above, from below, and from the sides in the organization. At this consistent position and having authority over the effective use of resources, this manager cannot rightfully say an individual under his charge made him fail or is the reason something did not get done. On a political level, the manager, not the individual, is accountable to the organization and upper management for any deficiency. The individual should be held accountable to the manager only, but this notion is used to encourage positive outcomes and growth of the individual, and not for the manager to use for self-serving, political reasons.

Not only from a point of view of what is right and wrong, but for better performance from individuals and teams, the manager should always give credit to others. This is required to build trust and promote loyalty of those for whom you are responsible. Your ultimate success is built on the many accumulated successes of others while you stay behind the scenes. The following passage from Benjamin Franklin's autobiography shows the value he found related to this idea. The quotation pertains to obtaining acceptance for his concept of a public subscription library, the first idea of a public library:

> The Objections, and Reluctances I met with in Soliciting the Subscriptions, made me soon feel the Impropriety of presenting one's self as the Proposer of any useful Project that might be suppos'd to raise one's Reputation in the smallest degree above that of one's Neighbours, when one has need of their Assistance to accomplish that Project. I therefore put my self as much as I could out of sight, and stated it as a Scheme of a *Number of Friends*, who had requested me to go about and propose it to such as they thought Lovers of Reading. In this way my Affair went on more smoothly, and I ever after practis'd it on such Occasions; and from my frequent Successes, can

heartily recommend it. The present little Sacrifice of your Vanity will afterwards be amply repaid. If it remains a while uncertain to whom the Merit belongs, some one more vain than yourself will be encourag'd to claim it, and then even Envy will be dispose'd to do you Justice, by plucking those assum'd Feathers, and restoring them to their right Owner.[2]

This is a good point in our discussion to introduce Overarching Principle #6:

Overarching Principle #6:

No trust or loyalty can exist without a two-way commitment to, and communication of, responsibility, accountability, and truthfulness.

The communication of the mutual and separate responsibilities of you and the individual is your responsibility as a manager and leader. You should always determine that the individual knows them well, and that he or she has accepted the role and tasks. You should always let the individual know your role in and around their responsibilities. This requires a great deal of dialogue and demands each be truthful with the other. Only then can you establish an infrastructure of trust and loyalty, as well as providing MEANING through Purpose and Relationship.

Knowing what is expected of him or her is not enough. You are to hold those who report to you accountable for their responsibilities, but that accountability is between you and that individual—period. If a deficiency were to exist in results, then it is up to you to work it out with the individual, and not use it outside your relationship for political reasons or personal gain.   If you were to take it outside the relationship, then you have not held up your part of the bargain.   Your responsibility is to support and help that individual in a collaborative manner to the limits of your abilities as his or her manager.

An important point needs to be made.   No matter how hard you want to help, never allow those for whom you are responsible to drop off a problem on you when it is within their responsibilities, even when they have to stretch in knowledge or skills to solve or overcome that problem.   Engineers-turned-manager have a tendency to take technical and non-technical problems alike off the hands of others, saying something like "no problem, leave the papers here, I will take care of it", or "let me take a look at it."   If you were to allow this, then you would become overwhelmed with work from all your reports, and you would be denying individuals a vehicle for growth.   You would confuse the division of responsibilities you mutually established; and, you would not have time to do the work that only you can do in the organization.   You should only take on problems from individuals when the obstacle or situation is at your level of authority in the organization and as manager only you should, or can, address.

Trusting the other person is critical in all this and requires an environment not poisoned by bending the truth, or flat-out lying, or questioning the veracity of others.   I was once an research engineer in a large corporation working in a small engineering group who supported in-house Ph.D. level scientists and engineers with designing and building their lab set-ups and pilot plants, and who developed mechanical designs used in company products.   I reported to a supervisor who was an engineer.   Just before starting with the company, I received my professional engineering license, my PE; an accomplishment of which I was proud and that meant a lot to me.   A few months into working with this particular supervisor, I learned he was a PE, so full of pride and camaraderie I told him I was a PE. He snapped back "no you're not." I was dumbfounded. I said, "yes, I am." He kept questioning me and denying that I could be. I kept trying to prove it, finally telling him to check the current roster of professional engineers that the state publishes. He ended it by having the last word, "I still don't believe it." I was emotionally deflated on many levels. Now, do you think this was an environment not poisoned by suspicion of lying or of open accusations against the credibility of subordinates? My statement of me being a PE was one of fact that was easily verifiable, but what of a statement not so verifiable involving complexity and judgment as so much of an engineer's work is? Added to this was his tendency to jump into a subordinate's project, taking over an interesting technical challenge for a short period, then afterward leaving one confused about responsibilities. By the way, I only reported to this supervisor less than one year before being transferred to another group in that company. I do not know whether this engineering supervisor ever grew to a level of leadership, but I did learn good lessons from him by learning what not to do. If you want trust and loyalty as a manager, you better trust your subordinates. Never assume the worse and always give the benefit of doubt. You can corroborate a story in many other ways, especially by following the ideas of Chapter 2, *Understanding, Before all Else*.

CHAPTER *5*

SPIRIT OF CHALLENGE

"Generally, in battle, use the normal force to engage; use the extraordinary to win... Now the resources of those skilled in the use of extraordinary forces are as infinite as the heavens and earth; as inexhaustible as the flow of the great rivers."

Sun Tzu, The Art of War
Translated by Samuel B. Griffith[1]

Routine is a large part of everyone's work. It adds value as customary practice in a trade or profession, operating procedures in an organization, and codes and standards in an industry. An individual or organization could not function at a high level of quality without routine; and quality is consistency by minimizing variation virtually through routine. How can efficiency be improved with any kind of work if not based on routine? However, routine has a negative connotation, notwithstanding that without it an individual could not make a living and an organization would not be able to function.

The negative connotation of routine comes from the fact that it is a characteristic of bureaucracy and red tape. What adds to the negative connotation is that within routine no change is possible, no innovation will occur, and those unaware of this circumstance become *stuck in a rut*. But even wheel ruts are valuable by making travel easier, quicker, and less risky by following the pioneers that went before. Change and innovation requires veering off out of the ruts, or from routine, into the wilderness and starting new ruts, or new routine. Still, the word routine creates a negative feel, but try to be efficient without it.

Usually one is forced out of routine when reacting to a problem that unexpectedly arises. The more urgent and significant the issue surrounding this problem, the quicker and farther from routine one is forced. This reacting is necessary, but not desirable. It is more desirable for you, as leader, to address change and innovation for the organization through projects and tasks that purposefully go beyond an individual's routine.

Certain functions of organizations by their nature should not involve work content that is routine, say as in research and development (R&D) or field service. Although, even these functions have routines in the work processes that may not stretch the individual, or the team. Change and the creation of new routines in work processes may be necessary for companies to create radically new products, to jump fundamentally in technology, or to discover vast new markets. Where organizations cannot innovate, it is where individuals are not being tested to think or to do beyond their current work processes, even if their very function is to create and innovate in work content, such as in research and development. Two companies of the same size and in the same industry could spend on R&D the same percentage of sales, but they do not necessarily have to obtain the same results for each R&D dollar. These results are not only in more new and improved products, but also in higher energy levels with more enthusiasm of its employees and its customers.

The work of the component of the leadership model JOB is about routine and the work of the component CHALLENGE of the model is about pursuing creative value for the organization by going beyond routine. The difference in the two is the individual takes on

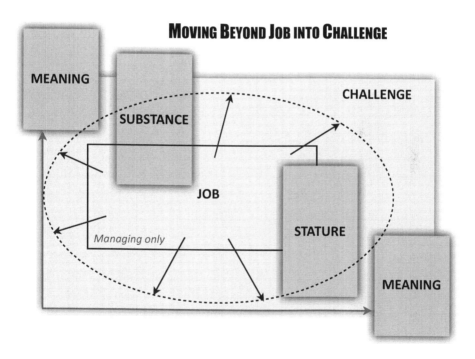

Fig. 5.1 Moving Beyond Job into Challenge. Shows individual leaving routine of JOB; model is unique for each individual for whom you are responsible or have an interest in their performance.

a technical or non-technical objective that involves personal risk when going beyond routine. His or her future becomes more uncertain, and it involves a factor of excitement that the individual may or may not enjoy. Routine is hum drum, status quo, and comfortable while CHALLENGE is scary, exciting, and full of opportunity. The individual is in the spotlight when in the realm of CHALLENGE, and will need the support and encouragement of you, his refined leader.

In addressing CHALLENGE, the individual goes beyond the usual tasks, activities, and expectations of JOB. Figure 5.1, *Moving Beyond JOB into CHALLENGE*, depicts the individual stretching, or in some cases being pushed, into CHALLENGE, represented by the largest rectangle. As explained, JOB and all other components of the model fit within any given CHALLENGE. The individual will need to step up to address CHALLENGE, beyond what is in JOB, to something more than his or her current Capabilities in skills and knowledge; to something more in Capacity from focus and effort; and to something more than Practice of the familiar where random events and the unexpected play havoc. The individual's SUBSTANCE and STATURE, as well as the leader's providing MEANING through Purpose and Relationship, become big factors of success within the encompassing larger region of CHALLENGE.

In CHALLENGE, solutions do not currently exist, and objectives are hard to define and more difficult to achieve. Through the work of CHALLENGE, the envelope is pushed in technology, efficiency, power, size, process, organization, or anything else for that matter that carries unknowns, risks, and uncertainties. Complications are ever present in CHALLENGE with many moving parts and with requirements of many and diverse stakeholders.

In addition to products, services, and technology, organizational change is associated with CHALLENGE. Having one's environment change is difficult for engineers and non-engineers alike.

The extent and rate of change has an effect on how individuals think, feel, and act. Success in change for an organization is directly connected to the commitment and energy level of all involved surrounding that change, and their acceptance of learning and of personal growth that lead to new routines.

ELEMENTS OF CHALLENGE

- Unexplored
- Chance
- Creativity

Breaking down CHALLENGE into three separate, but closely interrelated, elements helps you and I understand CHALLENGE better, and provides a means by which we can only hope to influence desired outcomes from multiple potential futures. CHALLENGE from the model is composed of Unexplored, Chance, and Creativity.

Leaving routine and known practice, creating something new, and making changes is moving into new territory, unknown and unexplored. Just how unknown and unexplored depends on the individual, or team, and how far they have to go off the beaten path, from start to finish. For an individual, simply learning something new is a form of exploring for that individual, even though many before have obtained the same knowledge. For an organization, new products, new methods, new markets, and change in general all involve Unexplored as it exists before CHALLENGE begins.

The probability of failure or success rests upon the unexpected; and how it is anticipated and acted upon. The unforeseen and unexpected can be anticipated, if not precisely, then in overall tendencies.

To succeed in CHALLENGE, the individual and team must know the handiwork of Chance, and her vagaries.

All change stems from Creativity, the third element of CHALLENGE. Allowing and promoting the conditions to exist for Creativity to occur is an essential part of refined leadership. Creativity as an element of the model, as well as the elements of Unknown and Chance, will be covered later in the chapter.

A FELLOWSHIP ENSUES

An unsophisticated image from popular culture of a boss prodding a subordinate to work and of a worker trying to avoid work, and maybe even trying to avoid the boss, implies people have the basic trait of laziness and must be forced to work. From my experience, this is not true, and when it comes to engineers and other technical professionals, I have found the opposite to be true. Provided the right work climate, individuals take initiative and work diligently. What is more, individuals want to provide a helping hand whenever they can, and if they are reluctant to help, then it has more to do with their response to poor management providing no leadership than it does with a poor work ethic.

Human nature is such that an individual can easily become enthusiastic about their work with the right conditions; that is why having a good work ethic and working hard is said to be healthy for an individual. It is part of our nature. Human beings, especially those with the talents and dreams that lead them into a technical profession or trade, exhibit a tendency to work hard when it means something to them, and to work even harder when they are part of something bigger than themselves. Work ethic, along with enlightened self-interest, underpins much of the refined leadership model.

In my most recent position as head of an engineering depart-ment, I had the good fortune and privilege to have experienced initiative and desire to help. On many occasions, an individual would come into my office volunteering to take care of it for me when having heard of an issue with which I was struggling, or a problem I needed solved, or a stray task that needed to be performed. The unsolicited response to take on more work to help from engineers and technical professionals, whose days were completely filled with their current workload, is evidence of my belief in the emergence of a fellowship around good leadership. This is expressed in the following overarching principle:

Overarching Principle #7:

A fellowship will arise around good leadership, especially to pursue a higher purpose and a call to challenge. In this environment, no one cares who gets the credit, making anything possible.

I can vouch for the fact that the phenomenon of fellowship occurs. I have seen it arise when a true team forms to achieve big objectives in the realm of CHALLENGE. A group can be said to be a team only when a fellowship exists, otherwise they are just a group. A team can be put together by management for a specific project, but it will exist in name only until a fellowship comes about. In a fellowship, each helps the other. One individual fills in gaps in skill or knowledge for another, while in turn that individual is helped and has his or her shortcomings covered by yet another. No one criticizes the next person. They just get done whatever needs to be done at that time. Fellowship is fostered by mutual goals and commitments, and by each being accountable to the others on the team. After the team has reached the point where individuals have bonded

through passing initial obstacles and solving the first technical difficulties, the team increasingly feels answerable to only itself, where
everyone else is on the outside, including management. This is especially true when the team members have been freed from their
routine responsibilities of the leadership model component of JOB.
The individuals on the team become fully energized beyond any
level a person who manages with no understanding of leadership
could imagine, let alone dictate.

Using a team is the best approach in attacking CHALLENGE. A
true team is not just a group of individuals thrown into a room. A
true team is the vehicle for pure collaboration involving inquiry,
imagination, synthesis, decision making, all else concerning creativity, and a whole lot of shared judgment. This is why cross-functional
teams are so prevalent today in modern organizations. However,
good outcomes from teams are not guaranteed, and to be successful,
good leadership is required. In Chapter 7, *Job and Organizational
Know-how*, teams are discussed further, the way to think about them,
and how to connect individuals.

Why is it important that nobody cares who gets the credit? I
have experienced a range of corporate cultures. When an Us-Them
environment exists, political factors kill creativity; and this is so because collaboration across functional groups occurs in a forced fashion, if at all. What little interaction there is, it is in a climate of distrust with individuals guarding information and new ideas. One
symptom of the Us-Them environment is the claiming of credit,
valid or not, that suits one party over another. This taking of undue
credit, as well as the placing of baseless blame for something that
might have gone wrong, occurs freely through disinformation. Focus is not on obtaining a successful outcome as a team with everyone
winning, but on politically seeking favor with management with per-

sonal winning as the goal. In a healthy true team environment, nobody cares who gets the credit.

ENGAGING WITH JOB, WINNING WITH CHALLENGE

The quotation at the top of this chapter is appropriate for bringing about novel products and change in an organization and for providing competitive advantage. The normal force, or conventional main force, *cheng*, is expected and usual, used generally to engage the enemy. However, the extraordinary force, *ch'i*, is unexpected and unusual, employed specially to defeat the enemy. The normal force gains the attention of the enemy, causing the enemy to react to it, while the extraordinary force strikes a blow elsewhere. The use of combination of the two involves constant maneuvering to distract the opponent, and finessing opportunities that arise for exploitation. The combination could transform, *cheng* becomes *ch'i* and *ch'i* becomes *cheng*, to exploit a favorable situation. This thinking comes from *The Art of War*, attributed to an ancient Chinese general, Sun Tzu.[2] I see JOB as *cheng*, and CHALLENGE as *ch'i*.

Current routine operations of a company, along with its current competitive stance, its products and product technology, and its current marketing, are analogous to the normal forces, or *cheng*. On the individual level, it is JOB that is similar to *cheng*, with its written position description, standard procedures, and customary practices, but most of all with its know-how. Analogous to *ch'i* are a company's new operating methods, new products and new product technology, and new markets and marketing. For the individual, *ch'i* is the stretching and moving beyond JOB with CHALLENGE, and the effort and vitality making up the project teams to deliver *ch'i*. Consider the competitive landscape in which companies satisfy their customers' needs with products and services. Competitors engage in the marketplace through consistency, routine execution, and high quality from low variation, while working secretly on changing that competitive landscape with the unique and novel results created by its teams and projects. *Ch'i* is competitive change, and it can only be brought about by CHALLENGE of the model, through projects and teams. Your extraordinary forces are your projects, teams, and individuals going beyond JOB with CHALLENGE.

By you going beyond managing the individual to leading that individual, and by repeating this with everyone who reports to you as a manager and with everyone with whom you work, you have the ability to convert *cheng* and *ch'i* to everyday actionable projects at a higher purpose. You make this personal for all by putting these ideas into CHALLENGE on a human level with each individual. It depends on how much you free up the individual from JOB to focus on CHALLENGE, and how well you frame the immediate goals to fit the higher purpose of the organization, especially in finding a competitive advantage to exploit in the marketplace. While the conventional main force of the organization engages the competition through collective JOB, maintaining current revenue streams and profits, separate effort of the extraordinary force through projects outside of JOB discovers how to move market, product, technology, and processes from their current state for entrepreneurial change and competitive advantage.

When an individual accepts a project to lead, it resembles a call to adventure for the classic hero from legends. The individual is thrust into unknown territory, uncertain of outcomes. He or she struggles to understand, to make sense of it all, and takes the necessary journey to find the answers. The hero overcomes deadly obstacles, testing courage and strength, exposing weaknesses and fears. The hero never knows what to expect or what success will look like, so he or she goes on faith. Always, the hero learns much about himself or herself, and grows. Does it sound like what you went through during your last project? Did you feel yourself becoming stronger with every new problem you solved and task you completed? The bigger and further the goals of what any individual accepts of the model element Unexplored, the more the experience will be like the hero's journey of legend. This will be when the real opportunity from CHALLENGE of the model becomes apparent, and where the real medium for personal and professional growth is found.

As a manager, you can see the necessity of excellence in routine, continuous improvement, control of variation, with consistency and no surprises. But as a leader bringing about change, you see the value in new ways of doing things, in quantum jumps in improvements, in promotion of variation through imagination, and in stirring the pot looking for beneficial surprises. For the individual and team to create change, variation is good for purposeful creativity and exploratory tinkering, quit different from business as usual. The more individuals are freed from their routine to focus on CHALLENGE, the less standard operations will be inadvertently and adversely impacted, and the more focus there will be to create change and new products, technology, or markets. In small companies, this is not easy and requires a commitment to view this as an investment in something new. The investment is also in the creation of spirit, vigor, and dynamism in those freed of their routine responsibilities to pursue CHALLENGE as an extraordinary force.

CONFIDENCE, PATIENCE, AND TIME

For an individual to succeed at a difficult task for which they stretch their abilities, he or she must endeavor under the right conditions and must be given the necessary support. Those conditions and support are the responsibility of the individual's manager. A good manager knows the circumstances and the surroundings that matter and knows the type and degree of support that needs to be provided. The elements of the refined leadership model are areas in which to focus in creating the conditions and providing support the individual needs to succeed.

A large part of providing support is showing confidence in and having patience with the individual working a knotty problem, a difficult task, or a protracted project. I defined CHALLENGE as the individual going beyond his or her usual tasks, activities, and expectations of JOB. How much the individual will need your support to stretch to address technical and non-technical tasks in CHALLENGE is dependent on the individual's SUBSTANCE and STATURE as measured against the difficulty of the problem, the attendant risks, and the extent of uncertainties. There are times when support for an individual in the process of growing takes on the form of a leap of faith that an individual can live up to the perception of their potential. In a small company with limited resources—or even in a large company considering there are never enough resources and scarcity is a fact of economic life—it becomes imperative to ask individuals to summon all they have to achieve big things. And they need all the benefits a manager acting with leadership can provide, starting with confidence and patience.

To create an energetic atmosphere in your area of responsibility, you need to provide MEANING for each individual and the appropriate level of CHALLENGE. In this way, you encourage learning and growth, you create excitement for that individual, and you address the risk of boredom. Never protect an individual by thinking they cannot do something because only you can do it, or it is easier to do it yourself. That will kill energy and excitement, learning and growth, team spirit and fellowship—cold.

Asking difficult questions, bringing up awkward facts, or discussing embarrassing issues in a constructive manner is healthy, but in private as discussed in Chapter 4 under a *Manner of Interacting*. This is your way of supporting the individual with your insight and experience, but it stays between you both, or members of the team. It is not for the consumption of those outside the leadership-individual relationship.   Any bad news or negative information should be provided to the appropriate stakeholders only, but not during the normal process of working the problems. Technical progress and innovation is messy, and not pretty at times, where the professionals involved need to discuss and work out details, test ideas and digest results, explore occurrences and solve interrelated problems, and come to fully understand before giving outside interests the opportunity to use politically any points of the messiness. You must express valid concerns openly with the individual, the team, upper management, and your peers, but do so while showing confidence.

This brings us to the one factor with which all human beings deal in order to be successful, and that is time:

Overarching Principle #8:

An acceptance that every activity
has a rhythm and a timing, and a sense of such,
is the basis for patience and perseverance.

Your confidence in the perseverance of others cannot be genuine unless you have patience. However, you cannot have patience when you have no sense of how long something should take to accomplish. Too often estimates become locked in concrete that were not realistic, influenced by factors unrelated to the reality of what has to be done. Even the best estimates do not accurately consider negative random events and the leadership model element of Chance. Outcomes when advancing the art, especially for breakthrough products or new technologies, are not predicable.

The timing an individual and a team take to reach a planned milestone is based on its nature, much as a pendulum, or a mass and spring system, has a natural frequency. You cannot force it to swing or oscillate faster without affecting its performance, just as you cannot ask an individual to have it done by tomorrow when realistically it takes no less than five days. If you could develop a sense of timing and rhythm for a project and people, you can be better at understanding the element of time, the bane of all project managers, executives, and investors alike.

I cannot provide you a step-by-step procedure for understanding the natural timing of any situation, or for any project, but I can say that progress is never linear and appearance of progress is never telling. I know the way I personally work that to an observer, especially one outside my head, I am not making progress at all in the beginning phases of my project. That is especially true for engineering work, one cannot see what is going on inside another's head. But foundations are being laid, ideas are gestating, outlines and structure are forming, observations and inquiry are building, and by all outward appearances, things are starting slowly. Only later do actions appear to others as accelerating in making progress. My best suggestion for sensing the appropriate timing is to follow the ideas of Chapter 2 to fully understand what it will take, how it will be done, and where the individual workers are in their progress. Never delude yourself if you should feel something is not right, or things do not add up, but know it is something you must understand further.

The attention of upper management to the progress being made for a given project will depend on the strategic importance to, and the financial impact on, the company. For projects where many unknowns exist, if at all possible, do not put the projected results of this uncertain project into the financial expectations of the company. One of my toughest times as a engineering department head was associated with a breakthrough product from which the potential sales and income was factored into the finances for company growth. Unrealistic business expectations and knotty technical and organizational issues made it a no win situation with me in the middle. This project was to develop a breakthrough product loaded with functions and features new to our company and new to the world. The market release schedule was based on optimistic estimates of the number of redesign cycles required based on success with the first prototype testing. The lead engineer and his technical team were overcoming obstacles one after the other through hard physical work with the prototype in the laboratory and with creative design solutions from the designers. My role was to insulate the technical team from political pressure from above and from all sides, while keeping everyone's enthusiasm and self-confidence at a required high level for such a project. In the end, we ran out of time when the owners ran out of patience. I understand the project was dropped, the company and the world did not have a breakthrough product based on new technologies, and I left with my dignity intact. The amount of innovation an organization will bring to market is directly proportional to the patience of those making the investment.

Timing is the critical ingredient for the execution of change, the effect on competitive advantage, and winning in the marketplace. Therefore, it is paramount in CHALLENGE to allow the rhythm of the project teams and the organization. Static schedules are like static defenses in battle; they do not provide fluidity and flexibility to be useful in reacting as needed. The further into the future activities and events are planned, the more uncertain they become, and the more flexibility is required. To obtain a sense of the direction a project is taking and how it is being accomplished, you need to use the leadership model element of Relationship. The best estimates for project status are bottom-up from those responsible, but confirmed by your understanding. Any estimates from planning should be consistent with your feelings and what you sense is, or is not, right.

You should know whether time is on your side or against you. What does this mean? If you do nothing, or progress stays on its current path, as time elapses in terms of the appropriate scale (hours, days, weeks, months, etc.), will you win, lose, or suffer no consequence? Use the breakthrough product project I just mentioned as an example. From the financial perspective in a time scale of fiscal quarters, clearly time was not on our side as long as no market introduction of the product occurred; but, from the perspective of developing new product technology and getting closer to a breakthrough product, time was on our side. If nothing were to change viewed at that point in time, we were on course to win technically, but were loosing based on the timing of the financial projections. Ultimately, a product new to the world would have been introduced to the market, but we ran out of time—the financial perspective governed as I sensed it did at the time. To determine whether time is on your side or not, determine what part of the situation governs.

ELEMENT: UNEXPLORED

Comfort zones, we all have them. Some enjoy going outside of their zones and into the Unexplored; they would be bored otherwise. For everyone, except a suicidal dare devil or a pathological gambler, there exists degrees of tolerance for risk and uncertainty ranging from an excursion into areas not too unfamiliar all the way to an unsafe, great unknown. But nonetheless, to exact change, to innovate, and to compete in business, one must venture afar. For those in the engineering community, that means new products, new technologies, new construction techniques, new manufacturing methods, and in general, technical, organizational and entrepreneurial change. With leadership on a human level, it means extending the responsibilities and objectives for that individual—and yourself—beyond the routine of JOB into Unexplored, one of the three elements of CHALLENGE. Unexplored is related to tasks, projects, and objectives not yet accomplished before, and those filled with risk and uncertainty. The greater the opportunity for the individual and the company, the more uncertain the outcome and the greater the risk assumed by both. Unexplored has to do with technologies and methods, with knowledge and skills, and with the next state along a line of progress.

Nothing can be more exciting for some technical professionals than when they are told they are needed to explore and create something new. Historically, this appears to be the nature of the human spirit, that is, adventure and discovery. An organization of individuals thus charged up, energized to come to work each morning, and unable to bear leaving at night, is the result of moving into new areas of Unexplored.

But for other individuals with not so adventurous personalities, they resist going beyond their basic responsibilities in their work, and to advance through accomplishment other than what is needed to get by, because of fear, uncertainty, and doubt. Remember F-U-D from Chapter 4 under *Manner of Interacting*. You can do much to make them feel they will not be penalized for failure. Mistakes and failures should be acknowledged, but framed within the attitude of nothing ventured, nothing gained. You must promote the conviction that in CHALLENGE we learn from our mistakes and by our failures, while it is necessary to guard against making fatal mistakes or producing big failures.

Taking risks and fear of failure are balanced by reward. I am sure European explorers of the sixteenth and seventeenth centuries who navigated an unknown world took the risk more for the potential reward of riches than for advancing knowledge. The assumption of risk and degree of uncertainty should be reasonably appropriate for the potential reward for the individual, the team, and the organization. In companies of today, the reward is the return from ultimately better satisfying a need, or unmet need, of customer or user, and this can be expressed in terms of the degree of change to the product (or service) plus the change to the processes around the product (or service). This can be expressed as follows:

- **Incremental** — a revision based on existing product or process and core technology with focus around routine of JOB — zero to low risk;

- **Derivative** — a modified product or process based on existing products and core technology with focus around a blend of routine of JOB and and Unexplored of CHALLENGE — low to moderate risk;

- **Platform** — a new product or method of manufacture or operation based on new or modified core technologies with a blend of routine of JOB, uniqueness of SUBSTANCE, can do of STATURE, and Unexplored of CHALLENGE — moderate to high risk;

- **Discontinuity** — a new category of product or unmet user need based on technological or market breakthrough highly dependent on SUBSTANCE, STATURE, and CHALLENGE for success — extremely high risk.

The project becomes increasingly more personal for individuals and teams going from Incremental to Discontinuity, and the managing style needs to go further from *managing only* to a refined leadership. In addition to each individual increasingly committing more of themselves to their project, cross-functional teams become paramount for providing the breadth and depth of perspective and skill to accomplish the more involved projects. At the Platform and Discontinuity levels, entrepreneurial perspective is a large component of the systems level thinking that is needed for success. Not only should the probability of technical success be considered, but also the probability of market success. The overall probability of success is the mathematical multiplication of the probability of technical success by that of market success (e.g., if 50% chance of technical success and 50% chance of market success, then total chance of success is 25%, not too good).

The area of study of technology management is useful in Unexplored. All products and their manufacture are the result of know-how, which can be thought of as technology. Any technology, or set of technologies, that go into the existence of a product, or service, is only expressed in the marketplace through that product. And what is more, the marketplace inspires advances in technology through the needs associated with the product, or service. The existing technology, or know-how, for existing products of quality manufacture (low variation) are firmly entrenched by routine. This routine is the individual's work in JOB. The further the jump in technology and from routine, the further the individuals move into Unexplored, and further they venture along the continuum of change from Incremental to Discontinuity. And the further toward Platform and Discontinuity, the better the organization's technology strategy has to be. Technology management as a discipline deals with just this.

Time is always a factor, and it is no different with Unexplored. The time required to be successful must match the level of change the project is expected to bring about. From an urgent need to correct a deficiency or an existing condition in the field to creating a new product category in the market, time is the primary variable to success. Speed-to-market techniques are harmful when they are only based on wishful thinking. Time constraints can decrease the probability of success by the need to get things done, and by prompting the exertion of more of the model element Power for an individual than normally would be required in the blend of STATURE and CHALLENGE by the team.

The further from the routine of JOB and the further the individual goes into Unexplored, the more the territory becomes unfamiliar. As the territory becomes more unfamiliar, the more SUBSTANCE and STATURE of the individual, as well as Chance and Creativity, contributes to success. The refined leader always provides extra support to the individual and team when they are in unfamiliar territory. With respect to possible failure in the many tasks and goals of a complicated and difficult project, the refined leader provides a safety net, along with the encouragement, to keep fear from being a distraction. The elements of the model of leadership provides the dimensions on which to focus to positively influence the atmosphere and spirit surrounding CHALLENGE.

ELEMENT: CHANCE

We learn to live with chance; it is ever present. It is the basis of all games, even games of skill; otherwise, if the outcome were known beforehand, it would not be a game. Chance governs man's existence and is the source of much hope and many disappointments. The vagaries of chance can be analyzed afterward, explaining failures and successes in all types of undertakings across all walks of life, especially throughout history. Chance has caused angst from ancient Roman generals at the frontier to Las Vegas poker players at the table, from small time politicians in local elections to heads of state in geopolitical politics, and from CEO's of corporations undertaking the biggest mergers to engineers developing the biggest ideas. Even when sizable resources are brought to bear by corporations, whole industries, and governmental regulatory agencies to guard against things going wrong, there are no guaranties. Chance has had its day from nuclear power plant mishaps to deep water oil drilling disasters. Anyone who does or creates anything deals with probabilities, and they experience random events from the operation of chance.

How do you think the following arcane equation affected you and many others on this planet?

$$\text{VaR}_\alpha = \inf\{l \in \Re : P(L > l) \le 1 - \alpha\} = \inf\{l \in \Re : F_L(l) \ge \alpha\}$$

This is the mathematical model for *value at risk*. Even to an engineer who uses mathematics in his or her work, it looks intimidating: hard to understand and tricky to apply. Do not worry, you will not be asked to use it; I only present it here to make a point. This equation represents a model that was the basis for the creation and explosive growth of the many innovative financial products from the financial industry that led up to the financial crisis of 2007-2008 and the resultant Great Recession. As the new financial instruments became increasingly more complicated and harder to understand, the value at risk model was used for the purpose of limiting risk of transactions and financial holdings. It provided the financial experts and executives with the confidence to leverage their businesses to high levels in dealing with these exotic and innovative investments. However, the assumptions made by the experts and the amount determined at risk were inadequate in describing the potential loss.

The experts did not allow for unusual events, in this case the collapse of the U.S. housing market. Home mortgages were a large part of the assets being securitized in these financial products sold around the world. As we have learned from past manmade disasters, any expert in any field of endeavor can get into trouble by not understanding the limits of their formal and tacit models, or by not putting enough weight in their thinking toward unknowns and the possibility of chance happenings.

The element Chance falls within CHALLENGE in the model of leadership. Chance is closely connected with the elements Unexplored and Creativity.

Chance is at the heart of risk and uncertainty. Having no risk or uncertainty means the following:

- to be able to predict *all* future events;
- possess *all* relevant technical knowledge;
- be cognizant of *all* interactions of *all* people involved, or lack thereof; and
- take preventative action for *all* potential negative events.

This is not likely for the best manager or engineers operating with resource and time constraints. Even with an unlimited budget, individuals and teams would have to predict all future events—still not likely. There will always be risk and uncertainty.

What is Meant by Risk

Risk is a potential loss from a possible occurrence of an unwanted event, such as a financial loss from a technical defect appearing in a new product, or a loss in production rate from a failure of a piece of manufacturing equipment. A potential event can be identified, and the loss quantified, by deliberate effort using creative thinking combined with experience from past similar occurrences. By asking "what can happen that we do not want to happen?" and "if this happens, what are the negative effects?," potential events and related negative effects can be determined and brought to the fore for preventative action. This characteristic of risk, that it can be identified and quantified through calculation of the probability of occurrence and the estimation of the degree of loss associated with that occurrence, makes it highly influenced by past experience and the ability to project thinking into the future. The quantification of probabilities and losses is dependent on whether one uses facts, assumptions, or something in between, but highly dependent on the mathematical or descriptive model used, and hence the need to pay close attention to the models one adopts and the assumptions one makes—to wit the value at risk equation and the assumption concerning home prices.

As an illustration of what is meant by risk and how it can be quantified, consider the promise by an engineering manager to a supply chain manager to have in his hands in one week by next Friday a released set of revised fabrication drawings for a subassembly used on one of the company's products. It is important for the supply chain manager to have these drawings, because he is placing the next purchase order for them on that Friday. The engineering manager knows there is the possible event that the revised drawings will not be released on time. After understanding most of the circumstances about the situation, the engineering manager puts an estimated probability of 3 in 10 on the possible occurrence that the revised drawings will be late. If the drawing were late, then the risk of not obtaining the savings of $10,000 with this purchase order to the supplier of the subassembly would be realized.

Once identified, a risk can be managed with preventative action and plans for contingency action. If you were to eliminate *all* possible causes of an unwanted event, you eliminate the potential for that event. However, one cannot address all possible causes, the list would be endless. Let us continue with the engineering manager of our current example. She decides the approximate 30% probability of failure to meet the date warrants attention. She decides the release of these drawings are important enough to ensure they are released on time. What can she do? She calls into her office the designer who is revising the drawings, sitting down at her small conference table, they discuss in a relaxed atmosphere what could go wrong. She guides the discussion about the possible causes for not meeting the date. The list is long, but the top three most probable causes are the designer relapsing into an illness he just recovered from days earlier, a host of computer system problems that have been occurring lately, and a technical problem they have been having with the material of construction of one of the parts in the assembly that may require a technical decision, thus delaying the work. From the long list, they chose together to address the most likely potential causes. Using the three most probable causes above, she asks a second designer to be a back up, and to stay informed on the work of the first designer in case he relapses into illness. She asks the IT manager to keep on eye on the computer system and to help with frequent file backup; and the designer confirms with the cognizant engineer working on the issue the suitability of the current material of construction, being assured no new request for use of a different material of construction was imminent. Since the risk is not large, that is, probability of occurrence is low and financial impact is small, she and the designer took less than thirty minutes to address the top three potential causes. The more important aspect of meeting the release date is the goodwill she wants to maintain by helping the supply chain manager who is her internal customer. Summarizing, risks can be identified, quantified, and somewhat managed by taking preventive action and having contingency plans.

The following are just a few examples of tools used in business and industry for risk analysis and prevention of loss:

- hedging stock market positions using call and put options
- protecting contract pricing in finance with exchange rate futures
- guarding against defects in design and manufacturing using FMEA's (failure modes and effects analysis)
- assuring quality from preventing variation using Six-sigma methods
- validating the reliability of product or process function using data from history, experimentation, studies, and trials

All of the above are based on models using statistical analysis and normal distribution (the bell curve). This means the customary and accepted tools available to deal with risk are based on routine and the continuous improvement of routine. It focuses on what has been done many times before. With CHALLENGE, the new routine is yet to be established, so uncertainty plays a larger role.

What is Meant by Uncertainty

I recall a funny cartoon I once saw in a newspaper. In the CEO's office of a financial investment firm, there is a person in a lab coat with the appearance of being tech support, hunched over a crystal ball on the desk. The CEO is asking if he could increase its range.

Of course, the CEO wanted to see further into the future to reduce his uncertainty. Because the more we know, are aware of, and can imagine, the less uncertain we are about events happening or not happening. Our example of the engineering manager releasing drawings on time is a simple situation. In the real world with bigger projects, with CHALLENGE further from JOB, situations are much more complex. When more people are involved across many functional areas at various levels of expert knowledge and experience, geographically separated or culturally different, technically pushing the envelope in Unexplored has more attendant uncertainties.

Uncertainty comes about from three categories of unknowns:

- a limitation of knowledge
- a limitation of awareness
- a limitation of imagination

A *limitation of knowledge* could result from the extent of supporting science or the degree of acquaintance with that science. It could result from the undue time and expense of obtaining important information. A limitation of knowledge could come about from the incompleteness of data or from the problem of using data through induction. A *limitation of awareness* could result from not knowing changes made by others or from poor communication. A limitation of awareness happens at hand-off interfaces between departments and companies. A *limitation of imagination* results from focusing too narrowly or from using analytical tools that are not broad enough due to specialization. Limitation of imagination could occur from fictitious constraints established by a mental model and assumptions or by not considering operation outside that model.

When my wife and I fly for pleasure, we like to take a particular airline that provides satellite TV for each passenger. By watching a favorite cable channel during the flight, the flight becomes more enjoyable and it seems much quicker. However, the TV's are annoyingly not reliable in operation and I in the air have felt glad the engines are more reliable than the TV's. It comes down to the degree of risk of loss: a TV failing in operation versus an engine failing. Because of this difference in risk, the airlines, engine manufacturers, insurance companies, and government safety agencies have reduced uncertainty associated with the engines through overcoming the limitations above with better knowledge, more awareness, and richer imagination. This takes investment, people, time, and dedicated effort to continuously improve engines as has happened historically in the airline industry. Faulty TV's have no risk other than unhappy customers—well, maybe they will get on it.

I see unknowns as being in two categories, what I call *hard unknowns* and *soft unknowns*. Hard unknowns are what you do not know associated with reaching levels of expert knowledge, skill, and the science. Hard unknowns can be reduced, but with much expense, time and effort by advancing the technology or the science from which you draw for your work. Soft unknowns are what you do not know, but could know with not much expense and little effort, such as becoming more aware or applying more imagination and creativity. The ideas discussed in Chapter 2 about increasing understanding and Overarching Principle #1 help reduce uncertainty caused by the limitations of knowledge, awareness, imagination.

Test Conclusions, Validation, and Chimera

I do not recall when I first learned this, but I have long accepted that in science one can only disprove a scientific theory, but not prove it. No matter how many experiments or how much experience confirm the validity of a theory, an experiment or an event can come along with results disproving it. This is the problem of induction which is of major consequence in risk and uncertainty. Induction is the thought process of reaching a conclusion of truth from observation of events and data, or from experience. This conclusion is then accepted as true for all future occurrences.

A proof or validation of goodness does not increase the safety from the occurrence of a negative event, or that an unforeseen event will never happen. Before the terrorist attacks on September 11, 2001, no commercial jet airliners were deliberately flown into tall buildings for almost 100 years of human flight. Collecting one more day of data on September 10 did not increase the proof something like that could never happen. More of the same data using the same mental model does not decrease uncertainty and may only give a higher level of false confidence. In addition to experience or data, it is important that one selects the right model for which to apply experience—formal or tacit—and to overcome the limitations of knowledge, awareness, and imagination.

Where does this fit in with CHALLENGE and Chance? Always ask yourself of information, data, and experience, what does this tell me about tomorrow? In validating products or deriving comfort in plans, be alert to data and information outside your experience or expertise. Usually the conclusions you arrive at from your experience are influenced by your world view, or by tacit mental models. The more the data from your experience or from testing fits your tacit mental model, the more it supports your conclusion, but your model may be too narrow or wrong. With respect to experience, consciously examine fact, distinguishing it from assumption. But above all, understand the conclusions of individuals for whom you have a stake. This brings us to Overall Principle #9:

Overarching Principle #9:

In order to improve conclusions and decisions,
expand the associated tacit model for the endeavor by relaxing
focus and specialization. No accepted truth is safe from new data.

There is a famous example that illustrates this. First year engineering students have been shown the video of the destruction of the

Tacoma Narrows Bridge. It was due to high wind in November of 1940, and it collapsed three months after it was opened to traffic. The bridge was nicknamed Galloping Gertie and is a testament to, and a dramatic example of, what could happen when the mental model and expert focus are too narrow and analysis to specialized. In this case, bridge design practice at the time did not consider thoroughly enough, if at all, the non-obvious effects of aerodynamics and frequency response of wind on the structure. After the collapse, bridge design practice expanded the awareness of and the focus on aerodynamics and vibrational analyses. It often takes a mistake, or a disaster, to provide learning, and usually it is from an unforeseen negative event.

Unlike a manufactured product, a full-size prototype of a bridge cannot be built and tested to validate the final design. Prototyping is important, but not a panacea. Even after product prototypes have been fully validated by laboratory testing and field trials, failures in service happen. Is this not the problem we just discussed of induction? Validation as practiced is based on the obtaining of more data. You become more confident about the predicability of the product's function, but has your test model considered and tested all possible conditions? So how do you increase confidence and certainty from the validation information or data you obtain?

The right model for the testing must be selected. The independent variables (the inputs) that fully simulate the operating conditions and the dependent variables (the outputs) that measure the function of the product or service are critical. Sometimes, even expert knowledge does not know all the variables to consider. An expert who is too specialized might not have systems level judgment, practical application knowledge, or know peculiarities in use to select the right model or a broad enough model. Most often it is a tacit mental modeling that unconsciously controls the validation process, and it is always at risk of being too narrow. It is natural for experts to overestimate their knowledge while underestimating the unknowns. Expert opinion that is constantly questioning itself is preferred over that which is always confident.

Boundary conditions, or operating parameters, need to be realistic. Will the product ever experience an environment in use that is outside the limits tested? Is the test unit seeing the same static and dynamic conditions that it will see in use? Are all the combinations of input variables simultaneously operating being considered? This last requirement alone may have thousands of combinations of the inputs, even before considering any dynamic operation of each input alone.

Expect random events

The unexpected occurs everyday. I stubbed my toe hard this morning, and not once but twice within fifteen minutes on the same leg of my bed. Did I plan on this, or could I have prevented it from happening? Did the first stubbing help in preventing the second? On both occasions, it was the furthest thing from my mind. This was a random negative event. In the business world, and in the world of any endeavor where people are trying to achieve results, it is the basis of Murphy's famous law: if anything can go wrong, then it will go wrong. One can never know the universe of possibilities in its totality of things that can go wrong—or can go right.

I remember another cartoon from a newspaper—you can see I am big on cartoons. Picture three or four laboratory researchers standing around and looking into a beaker, one researcher saying that it was OK they didn't create life, but they did create a kind of glue or varnish or gum or something. It reminded me of the story of Post-it Notes from 3M Corporation, where the company discovered a weak glue-type substance, but they had no application. It took a separate event some time afterward for someone to make the connection with a use. The story of Post-it Notes is instructive, I recommend you read about it. It has been written about widely. My point with the cartoon is this: unexpected events will occur, no matter how expert or disciplined you are. What is important for success in leadership, however, is how you deal with the unexpected.

Random events can be positive and negative. When a random event occurs during a project, or in association with an individual with whom you are working, it will produce a result to your advantage, providing a benefit in some way, or to your disadvantage, causing a loss through realizing a foreseen or an unforeseen risk. This requires an asymmetry of response by you. Collect and amplify the good that is associated with the positive random event, and ignore or mitigate the bad associated with the negative random event. You should look for positive random events to build upon. Never let the effects of a negative random event grow. The potential occurrence of positive random events is why for creativity and innovation you want to stir the pot to promote randomness, breaking fictitious restrictions. Surprises from the real world generate more alternatives and ideas than just relying on imagination alone.

This brings us to the next overarching principle:

Overarching Principle #10:

Distinguish between negative and positive random events, searching actively for the positive random events, learning from them and using them to your advantage.

When working with individuals and teams on projects, you and others, together or separately, will encounter many unforeseen and unpredicted occurrences and associated phenomena. Investigating and coming to explain the ones that were mysterious at first can be rewarding in providing revelation. I suggest you consciously and continuously look for positive random events; it will make each of your days at work an exploration of the world, no matter how mundane the work.

Of course, the opposite side of the flipped coin also occurs, the negative random event, despite your efforts at prevention by carefully trying to anticipate them. When unwanted unexpected events occur, however, address them aggressively, assess their degree of importance and urgency, and take corrective action. Most importantly for you and for the individuals for whom you are responsible, learn from them. Look at it this way, why else did they happen, except for you to learn? Nonetheless, guard against dwelling on the negative events. Instead, dwell and focus on the positive random events and the benefits derived from them.

Niccolo Machiavelli in his classic *The Prince* in 1513 wrote about the affect of fortune in human affairs. The following paragraph illustrates the interplay of human intervention and unexpected events. The *her* he refers to is Fortune:

> I compare her to one of those raging rivers, which when in flood overflows the plains, sweeping away trees and buildings, bearing away the soil from place to place; everything flies before it, all yield to its violence, without being able in any way to withstand it; and yet, though its nature be such, it does not follow therefore that men, when the weather becomes fair, shall not make provision, both with defences and barriers, in such a manner that, rising again, the waters may pass away by canal, and their force be neither so

unrestrained nor so dangerous. So it happens with Fortune, who shows her power where valour has not prepared to resist her, and thither she turns her forces where she knows that barriers and defences have not been raised to constrain her.[3]

He continues to argue that a prince who relied only on good fortune to be successful, one day will be happy and the next may be ruined if fortune were to change. He believes also "that he will be successful who directs his actions according to the spirit of the times, and that he whose actions do not accord with the times will not be successful." In the case of the philosophy of leadership being presented in this book, your plans and actions cannot be independent of unexpected negative and positive random events.

One can use the tools of science, engineering, failure mode and effects analysis, Six-sigma methods, and lean manufacturing, but one should know their limitations in the world of surprises and the unexpected. They all are affected by the model used and the negative effects of expert knowledge. The weakest links for managing risk are uncertainty due to randomness and unknowns due to limits of knowledge, awareness and imagination. The closer to routine of JOB, the more successful the approaches just mentioned will be. The occurrence of the raging river, once the past event reveals the possibility, makes preparation for the future event much easier.

Control is illusory with Chance

A manager with a controlling style, one who is said to be a micromanager, and one who considers his or her reports an extension of himself or herself, may appear to be in control of his or her own destiny. In reality, it may be true for only the relatively small action areas where he or she knows what to do from what was learned from the experience of having done it many times before.

Getting to Point B from Point A with no variation from the initial plan and with no surprises, big or small, may become increasingly more probable as the objectives match experience through routine of JOB, and as the timeframe shortens and as the situation with participants and stakeholders is as it has always been. However, unexpected random events can affect those working to control their idea of perfection at the detail level. Once shaken from routine, a controlling manager enters the realm of CHALLENGE. The associated commanding and demanding nature of the micromanager loses the fellowship of others in indirect proportion to the dominating behavior and the negative feel associated with tight control. So in CHALLENGE, the micromanager has no ready access to a true team of individuals and the benefit of their SUBSTANCE, STATURE, and their Creativity, all positively influenced by MEANING.

Refined leadership is more effective than a controlling style of leadership when dealing with Chance. Reducing risk and uncertainty is not easy for any one person with the perspective of one person. It requires a better approach to understanding through a collaborative exercise. Moreover, it requires the bottom-up decisions and actions of individuals more cognizant and familiar with details than the controlling manager. Utilizing true teams with the required composite skill set is the opposite of a controlling manager calling the shots. It is like the difference between driving a power boat or sailing a sailboat. One does not have to be attuned to the subtleties of the wind, currents, and best direction with the one craft, but with the other, one must be accustomed to adjust continually to the dynamics of any situation. This, along with the fellowship, creates higher probabilities for better outcomes than for one person in total control obliviously powering his boat forward, no matter how expert that person.

Not using a command-and-control approach, or not micromanaging, does not mean you do not have an influence on the actions of others or the decisions being made. And it definitely does not mean you are not able to mitigate the effects of negative random events or to capitalize on positive random events. As a leader, you should always understand as much as needed of the big picture and of the details through appropriate interactions with people. With understanding, you should provide MEANING by reasserting Purpose and being active through Relationship. You should have a big part in affecting the individual's Standards and Capabilities, Responsibilities and Practice, Autonomy, emotional state, and Power. All the leadership elements are there for you to have an influence, even though you are not controlling.

Do not drive yourself and others into a frenzy over perfection in the details, usually the objective of the micromanager and one who needs to control. As you reach acceptable results, trying to get even better results takes increasingly more energy and time. This brings us to the next overarching principle:

Overarching Principle #11:

Because of randomness, limited resources, and time, nothing in life or work is perfect, and if it were, nothing would stay perfect; therefore, define perfection realistically.

By not embracing uncertainty and the importance of random events, risk is increased, despite tight control. Perfection in the form of unrealistic objectives with respect to resources and time becomes wishful thinking and denial, especially anytime someone disregards and ignores the unexpected. Any variation from what you expected should be investigated by using the ideas of Chapter 2. Not doing this is a missed opportunity and a danger at the same time.

Put Factors of Safety into Projects

Design engineers are familiar with the concept of factor of safety, where the size of a given factor of safety is governed by judgment of the designer based on the amount of unknowns that exist for the design of a product, machine, or structure. Unknowns come in many forms. Unknowns exist in mathematical models represented by design equations, or they lie with imperfections in the materials of construction. Variations in fabrication, manufacture, construction, and installation introduce many unknowns for the designer, as do assumptions made for operating conditions, such as forces, temperatures, and pressures. Predicting the potential misuse of the product by the user may require a factor of safety for the design of the product. So the design engineer decides on factors of safety for various parameters, smaller factors for those areas that have been tested or where there is experience, and larger factors for those areas new and untried.

I propose putting factors of safety into projects in much the same way as design engineers put them into their creations. This will require you to try to have a say upfront in a project. You can have an influence in the feasibility of the endeavor by putting in those factors of safety. The question then becomes how can we add factors of safety for projects associated with CHALLENGE and Chance? Figure 5.2, *Factors of Safety for Endeavors*, outlines how the refined leader can influence this in practice. My experience in business and industry has taught me that a *market need* or *product idea* usually grows in complexity and scope in organizations. If at all possible, keep the objectives for market need and product ideas simple, by not only resisting what is known as *scope creep* in organizations, but more importantly by making it simpler at the outset. The more fundamental the need, and the simpler the product, and the less conditions as restraints or qualifications on its use, then the more its entrepreneurial value.

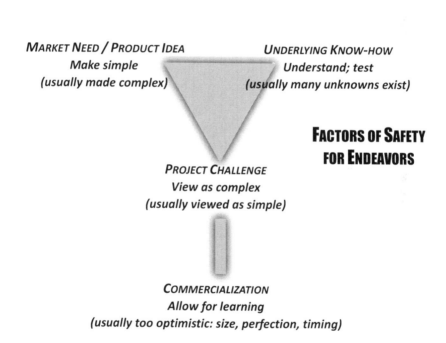

MARKET NEED / PRODUCT IDEA
Make simple
(usually made complex)

UNDERLYING KNOW-HOW
Understand; test
(usually many unknowns exist)

FACTORS OF SAFETY FOR ENDEAVORS

PROJECT CHALLENGE
View as complex
(usually viewed as simple)

COMMERCIALIZATION
Allow for learning
(usually too optimistic: size, perfection, timing)

Figure 5.2   Factors of Safety for Endeavors. Four areas the leader can influence a project from the point of view of expectations, available technology, and structure of the venture.

In addition to the objective of the product, the estimation of *underlying know-how*, that is, the knowledge and proven technology that enables the creation of the product, is usually wrong. There are most often than not an overestimation of the capabilities of the organization and an underestimation of the unknowns that exist. Therefore, understand as much as possible (see Chapter 2) and test what you know before starting the project.

With respect to the *project challenge* itself, or the component CHALLENGE in the model of leadership, those in organizations usually view this as simple, no problem, we did this before. Most of the time it is oversimplified by those not aware by describing it inaccurately as *exactly the same as* a so-and-so product. I say to put in a factor of safety, and view it more complex as you may first think.

At *commercialization*, organizations are usually too optimistic about the size of the market, the degree of perfection of the product, and the timing for acceptance and market penetration. With a new platform or discontinuity breakthrough product, the market itself has to be created. For an increased factor of safety for commercialization, allow for learning for all functional departments of the organization: engineering, sales, marketing, field service, manufacturing, replacement parts. And of course, be well prepared for unexpected negative and positive random events.

ELEMENT: CREATIVITY

There are many books available on the subject of creativity; I have accumulated and read quite a number through the years. The purpose here is not to repeat what has been presented so well elsewhere, and not to provide techniques for the creative process itself. My purpose is instead to show the leader's effect on the creative frame of mind and impact on innovative output for the organization.

With respect to the refined leadership model, Creativity, the model element, falls under CHALLENGE on the same level and alongside Unexplored and Chance. Creativity is coupled with Unexplored, it being Creativity's very environment, and is governed by Chance. Even where there is a good method to enhance creativity in the general sense, there is always a probability that an idea, or the sequence of ideas, that leads to invention will never be discovered.

The routine and focus of an individual's work within JOB inhibits the broader perspective required for creative thinking within CHALLENGE. Not only does everyday focus in familiar work form and shape fictitious restrictions when trying to find a few new and workable ideas, it blocks the ability to overcome these thinking constraints on imagination and to broaden the definition of the problem at hand. It becomes difficult *thinking outside the box* as the familiar phrase goes, or *thinking outside the dots* from the puzzle of the nine dots.

You probably already know the *Game of Nine Dots*. It is an excellent example of how fictitious thinking interferes with the creative thought process. On a sheet of paper arrange three rows of three dots, making a three dot sided square. To win, the objective is to draw straight lines through every dot without lifting the pencil from the paper. It turns out it is impossible if you were to make the unconscious assumption that you cannot go outside the square, or box, made by the dots. This is the fictitious restriction that needs to be overcome to win. In the realm of CHALLENGE requiring the element of Creativity, the individual must think *outside the JOB*.

As a manager or an engineer, you cannot command creative results in the same way that you cannot command that no negative random events will occur. You can only establish the conditions for creativity to happen by influencing the frame of mind of those involved by their immediate physical surroundings, their stress due to business ramifications, and their social interactions with individuals in a group or team setting. Using the leadership model, you affect the creative atmosphere through MEANING, SUBSTANCE, and STATURE, especially the emotional impact from Purpose, Person, Autonomy, and Importance. The model element of Power might have an inverse relationship with a creative atmosphere. Also, fear of failure and its consequences are particularly detrimental to fostering the ability of the human brain to perform in the higher functional regions required for the creative process.

To illustrate, consider different approaches by two managers to the same situation. Company XYZ has just discovered a problem with its products, a hand tool for the automobile servicing and repair industry. The problem has the potential of causing the company to lose market share to competition. The CEO has requested a redesign and revision to the product as soon as possible. A mechanical design engineer familiar with the product has been assigned to find a solution that may require a fair amount of creativity. All eyes, including the CEO, are on the engineer. No one in the company or along the value chain up to that point has had any good ideas as to how to design out the problem. This work can be considered outside the engineer's regular Responsibilities of JOB, out of his routine, and into the realm of CHALLENGE. He is struggling with finding a solution. Let us compare the different ways two hypothetical managers of the engineer handle this situation that result in two different outcomes with respect to the individual finding a creative design solution.

The first manager assumes and wants a rapid fix with accelerated timing, tells the engineer it is do or die for the company and do or die for the engineer. The manager is one who wins in any way he can and will not lose because of this engineer. He tells the engineer that if he fails, he would be the cause of making the manager look bad. All the while the engineer is working on the problem, the manager is intimating that he does not know why he assigned the engineer since he does not believe he is creative. The manager keeps walking over to the engineer's cubicle, keeps leaving voice messages, asks others to check up on the engineer and report back to him. The engineer's peers kibitz saying the current inklings of ideas will never work, it has all been tried before. These peers of the engineer have been overheard talking to the manager on the subject without the engineer present. The manager goes around saying the engineer should have known this would happen or should have designed it out before others found the problem, so the whole problem is his fault to begin with. The manager tries to force the engineer to work harder and longer in just the same way the manager likes to work. The manager keeps saying the engineer's efforts on this problem are keeping himself from working on more important projects.

The second manager assumes the correction of the problem with the product will take some time, so he clears it with the CEO to not rush the engineer working on the fix, especially since a creative solution, along with testing, will take time. He gives the CEO a realistic time frame. The manager then explains to the engineer that since the project is of such importance to the company, he has more time. In any case, the manager tells the engineer not to worry, that he, the manager, is there to help and support him as needed. He tells the engineer he has faith in his abilities for he has seen him succeed in tougher technical situations. He tells him don't worry if your first prototype needs to be modified, we need to explore creative solutions to beat the competition with this product anyway, so this is a competitive opportunity. He assures the engineer he is the best person to handle this, and explains to him why with valid reasons. The manager does not pester the engineer, but lets him know he can call or stop by at any time; and to please keep him informed on his progress. He asks the engineer's peers to help wherever possible, for this is a critical project, and to run their ideas by the engineer. The manager insists that anyone with ideas meet directly with the engineer and not with him in the absence of the engineer. The manager assures the engineer that problems occur with products in the field all the time, and it is how you respond that matters, so do not concern yourself with the past, except from which to learn.   The manager builds a stronger relationship with the engineer, learns more about him, and encourages him to draw on his unique background and talents in his hobby of working on cars. The manager emphasizes that he does not know who would be more qualified for this opportunity because of this hobby. The manager at his level of the organization influences resource allocation to support the engineer, to reassign appropriate resources, and to assemble a team.   The manager encourages the latest thinking of not just fixing the problem, but of finding a new concept that would be innovative for this product.

I do not have to tell you which manager has increased the probability the engineer's success in finding and implementing a creative improvement to the product, and may even be innovative for the industry. The next overarching principle follows:

Overarching Principle #12:

Innovation is encouraged by and is made possible through supportive, collaborative exploration, and with a desire to learn from failure.

The interaction of the first manager with the engineer in our illustration did not conform to this principle, or to the refined leadership model; that of the second did. With a relaxed atmosphere where failure was allowed, with a feeling of importance and independence, with the building of self-confidence, and with encouragement to draw on unique talents, the engineer, and those helping, were allowed room for Creativity, to roam Unexplored, and to let Chance work.

Improving creative outcomes

Creative thinking has as its fundamental unit the individual, and builds from there with two or more individuals in synch. An approach to creativity for me is a matter of being accustomed to thinking expansively by overcoming mental barriers, and then thinking critically to reduce the focus area to some promising ideas for further expansive thinking around those ideas. Both kinds of thinking will go on like this during the creative process in an alternating fashion. That is, one alternates thinking, first expanding the number and complexity of ideas using imagination and brainstorming techniques, then contracting the number and simplifying ideas using analytical and critical thought processes. For the creative individual and within the one brain, this process happens during long thought periods in flashes, but it is conjured up by a conscious effort to find an idea fit for the need. Like anything else, practice in thinking in this manner makes one better in creative thought.

The engineer leader who understands the creative thought process, especially if that engineer leader were well practiced in creative thinking, will know how to ensure the atmosphere for the individual is not intrusive on thought. Have you ever gotten *in the zone*, a state of such intense focus on your work that you become oblivious to time and of anything else happening around you? I have heard it called being in a *state of flow*, not aware of surroundings while ideas flow quickly and easily. This mental state does not have to be just for creative work, but for any type of work involving concentration. As an engineer, writer, artist, poet, cook, or daydreamer, you would have experienced this phenomenon.

The creative thought process is no different for a dyad (two people) or for a larger group. Each individual in the group, or team, should be comfortable with the creative process in order to contribute, but also in order not to disrupt the flow of the group. An advantage a group or team has over an individual in being creative is a synergy of thought and of the creative process. Synergy during the creative process is where one says one thing, triggering for another person a new idea in a different area of solution space, which in turn gives another an idea to another person, like a pin-ball machine. Ideas interact, connections are made, and images bounce randomly from pin to pin in the pinball machine of creativity, *bing-bing-bong-bing*... lights flashing... *bing-bong-bing*... "I got it!" Building on each other's thinking is synergy, that is, the creative output is greater when obtained by more than one person than the sum of each individual's creative output, if each worked alone.

A single individual can obtain a creative synergy alone over time. If enough time were to pass between creative sessions, the previous thoughts and ideas become cold, bringing about a detachment so the ideas lose their familiarity and appear to have come from another individual. This is much like proof reading one's own written work. For a group, synergy is obtained instantly from each other, for the individual it is over time.

The right atmosphere is important for an individual to be creative, but for a team, it is a necessity. When the team is made up of creative individuals in their own right, then it is much easier for you as leader to bring about a creative atmosphere. But when you are counting on the creative synergy of the team with internal adversity or with participants who are not practiced in creativity, you may be disappointed unless you can foster positive attitudes and emotions with strong facilitation.

The creative climate is brought about by concentrating on the elements of the refined leadership model that have the most effect. Below shows which elements are critical and why:

- MEANING

  - **Purpose**:   motivate through a higher purpose; affects many in company or society; bigger than the individuals involved; not just for pay or bonus

  - **Relationship**:   inspire individuals; understand situation and circumstances; communicate two-ways; provide encouragement and support; influence positive environment; assign credit where due and discourage distrust between individuals and groups; spur healthy and above-board competition; above all, prevent negativity, intimidation, or fear

- CHALLENGE:

  - **Unexplored**:   show as adventure; create excitement in the unknown; inspire by being the first; put in historical context; learning and gaining of knowledge; couple with Purpose in providing great meaning

  - **Chance**:   accept and let known always a chance of failure, do one's best; downplay consequences, minimize fear; stir up the unexpected to seize on positive random events

- SUBSTANCE

  - **Standards**: influence motivation and innate conscientiousness to achieve; perseverance; attitude on failure and success; acceptance levels of quality in work; value put on interaction with others; attitude on learning

  - **Person**: encourage drawing on unique background, training, skills, and knowledge; contacts and connections outside organization; what individual cares deeply about; family; cultural background; hobbies, interests, talents; uniqueness; how sees self; work with emotional make-up and personality, in general; cross-fertilization from other fields, cultures, and languages

  - **Capabilities**: coach on technical and professional skills, knowledge, and judgment; applied to JOB and outside needs of organization; ability to learn quickly; desire to learn other skills

- JOB:

  - **Responsibilities**: tie creativity to expectations; draw on skills and knowledge specific to JOB; expand from this as base into Unexplored

  - **Practice**: help separate from routine and rules that inhibit expansive thinking due to fictitious restrictions; help change or remove misleading assumptions; deal with constrictive nature of the authoritarian dominance of established patterns and procedures

  - **Capacity**: allot time for CHALLENGE beyond JOB; allow individual to be part of self-directed team

- STATURE:

  ‣ **Autonomy**:   allows freedom to work as individual works best; balance against routine of Practice; couples with feelings of Importance; couples with the elements of SUBSTANCE; allow freewheeling

  ‣ **Importance**: influence good feelings about individual's self; individual feels project has significance; affected by MEANING; build confidence

  ‣ **Power**:   make part of a game; allow playfulness; inject tactics and strategy; play to win despite permitting failure (a dichotomy with allowing failure, but work to succeed as failure is not an option)

A leader that emerges in the form of department head, engineering manager, engineering supervisor, project leader, project engineer, lead engineer, or engineer has the obligation through that leadership to promote the creative environment for the success of all. The leader should never claim credit. In a synergistic team situation, it is not even possible to know how an idea evolved. At all times, it is the individuals and teams that must get the credit despite your involvement or effort. Only then the individual will give fully of themselves and their ideas. Your reward will always be in the indirect fruits of a leadership well done, and the sharing in the success of the organization.

In a culture of cutthroat competition where workers seek the recognition from and the praise of upper management, trust is a rare commodity and no useful creative output is likely. The synergistic, collaborative process described earlier is not possible when individuals will not share partial, unformed ideas for others to build upon. In an environment where an individual sees others blatantly adopting and claiming his or her ideas for political advantage while at the same time being denigrated, no useful creativity is possible. An Us-Them environment with departmental silos and company-wide political infighting is fatal to innovation and growth. Any leader should not tolerate this type of injurious and crippling culture. This diseased culture is the opposite of one with a healthy climate of competition where individual's efforts are naturally distinguishable and attributable to that individual and to their team without the pettiness of a clamoring for credit.

For creativity to run its course, time plays a big factor. First, sufficient incubation time must be allowed for thoughts and ideas to germinate. Second, and as mentioned previously, adequate detachment must be achieved by letting previous thoughts and ideas become cold, somewhat forgotten. Third, ample patience must be present from the business. This usually is only possible if the leader, and the leader's management, were to fully understand the situation and circumstances around given projects and the affect on good creative results. Overarching Principle #8 is operative here.

Many of the points brought out in earlier chapters and sections of this chapter apply to the model element of Creativity, such as the following: questioning assumptions; broadening, restating the problem; relaxing focus and specialization; and seeing differently from another perspective. In addition, a creative process would benefit from using all the senses available to human beings—by using stimuli from sight, smell, hearing, touch, and not so easy, taste. You can find all this in the literature on the subject of creativity.

Characteristics of creative activities do not conform to the business-like planning and expectations of organizations. The following list is a summary of how projects, and creatively oriented work, can get into trouble in industry:

- Discovery of ideas not linear, starts and stops, messy

- Progress appears non-existent at times to others

- Motivation and energy flags with slow and inconsistent successes

- Objective may be modified during process, others see digression and regression (Purpose should not change)

- When is *good enough* enough to lock in the solution?

Projects of pure imaginative creativity, as in the arts, would not be useful in an industrial or commercial setting. The work product that results from when pure imagination is its only component is useless to business and industry unless it fits or satisfies a need. That brings us to the idea of the degree of fitness from Creativity.

Finding the hidden passage

Output from creative effort is required to satisfy a purpose and an intended function. Imagination is balanced by a practical goal. This purposeful creativity requires a blending of a determined method with chance. An art piece exists to be different, whereas an innovative product, or service, not only succeeds by differentiating itself from the competition, or by being new, but by finely satisfying a business purpose. It also has to function, and this requires a higher level of creativity; higher than, say, expressing oneself on a blank canvass and emotionally deciding its value. That is why creativity in an engineering setting requires involvement from a special kind of leadership. The output must be *new*, must *function*, and be *profitable*, while satisfying the *interests* of a large number of diverse stakeholders.

Imagination with a purpose paradoxically requires order. Pure imagination expands to disorder; that is its value. Conforming to a purpose contracts to more order, and again we find value, but of a different kind, that of a specific need being satisfied or a particular problem being solved. Through analytical and imaginative thinking, and physical tinkering, ideas expand and contract toward an embodiment that is created for a purpose. The process finds fitness.

Using an analogy of a mountain as the measure of fitness, a product or service can move to higher levels of fitness for a need in many attributes that make up the product or service. Creativity and new product development is like finding the passage that takes you to those higher levels on that mountain slope of fitness, getting ultimately closer to the summit. One problem is that you cannot see the passage and there are an infinite number of potential paths you can follow. Not being able to see a path ahead of you, or adjacent paths, you fumble as if you were walking in the dark up the slope. You reach dead-ends and have to go back time and again. There are obstacles to overcome, and you sometimes fall a short distance downward creating a slight setback, or you fall a great distance downward killing yourself and the project. For a company that has a viable, profitable, safe product that the customer needs and wants, many have been walking and climbing for a long time up many paths in an evolutionary way just to be at this point on the mountain slope. The pure artist using imagination only can stay at the bottom of the slope, far from the mountain peak of functional fit. A breakthrough product is one that has made its way up to a differentiating level of functional fitness, or that has jumped to a new and higher fitness mountain by the innovators' efforts.

Without learning from failure, none of us could find the hidden passage up to the higher levels of a product being suitable for an intended use. Random events, negative and positive, help in learning and in driving one up the slope on available passages, as more paths expose themselves. This is one reason why a good source of innovation is found where the most tinkering can occur easily and where it is closely associated with routine of JOB.

The following is an apt quotation from Charles Darwin's *The Origin of Species*. He is describing man's ability to use variation in animals to change the species to fit the desired purpose and needs:

> But when we compare the dray-horse and race-horse, the dromedary and camel, the various breeds of sheep fitted either for cultivated land or mountain pasture, with the wool of one breed good for one purpose, and that of another breed for another purpose; when we compare the many breeds of dogs each good for man in different ways; when we compare the game-cock, so pertinacious in battle, with the other breeds so little quarrelsome, with "everlasting layers" which never desire to sit, and with the bantam so small and elegant; when we compare the host of agricultural, culinary, orchard, and flower-garden races of plants, most useful to man at different seasons and for different purposes, or so beautiful in his eyes, we must, I think, look further than to mere variability. We cannot suppose that all the breeds were suddenly produced as perfect and as useful as we now see them; indeed, in many cases, we know that this has not been their history. The key is man's power of accumulative selection: nature gives successive variations: man adds them up in certain directions useful to him. In this sense he may be said to have made for himself useful breeds.[4]

The variability for selection by those developing new products or services comes from tinkering, from unexpected surprises through random events, and from ideas using imagination. Selection in this case is the effort of the individuals and teams for whom you are responsible finding the right path for a particular product improvement or creation. Continuing with the mountain analogy, the selection process is the search for the hidden passage up the slope toward the mountain peak of fitness.

You can use all the methods available to you to increase the probability of reaching your creative goal, but you have no assurances of success. Using the elements of the leadership model as a guide and using refined leadership as an approach, you will improve the odds when entering the realm of CHALLENGE.

CHAPTER *6*

SUBSTANCE OF THE INDIVIDUAL

"But the essential features of that individualism which, from elements provided by Christianity and the philosophy of classical antiquity, was first fully developed during the Renaissance and has since grown and spread into what we know as Western civilization—are the respect for the individual man qua man, that is, the recognition of his own views and tastes as supreme in his own sphere, however narrowly that may be circumscribed, and the belief that it is desirable that men should develop their own individual gifts and bents."

Friedrich A. Hayek, The Road to Serfdom[1]

There is an intense scene in the 1957 movie *The Bridge on the River Kwai*[2], where actor Alec Guinness, playing the commanding officer of British soldiers recently arrived in a Japanese prisoner of war camp in Burma, confronts the Japanese commander of the camp. The Japanese commander has just finished addressing the prisoners, informing them that they all will be working on the completion of a strategic bridge. After the main group marches off and the officers remain, Guinness discovers that the officers are also required to work on the bridge. He politely and with business-like efficiency explains that is not possible, because officers are not required to work according to the Geneva Convention. He pulls out a small book, dog-eared and by its poor condition appears well read. He opens to the appropriate passage, when the Japanese commander slaps it out of his hands. They both insist on their position, creating an impasse. A truck drives up, the back door drops down, a machine gun is revealed as it points at Guinness and the officers. The Japanese commander asks will they work, and Guinness says no. The commander starts counting down from ten. The count is at three, but the British commander is standing tall at attention, not backing down in the face of the machine gun. How does he resist, and why? What aspects within this individual are stronger than his fear?

In understanding Guinness's strength and reasons for his decisions in this scene, the model of leadership can be used. Was his course of action because of MEANING? In particular, was it Purpose, willing to die for his country, or Relationship, having a bond with his officers, his men, and his superiors? His position could have come from CHALLENGE, chancing to cause a positive event to better their situation for survival, and possibly contribute to winning the war. Or could it have been because of JOB, having his Responsibilities as a commanding officer, or in Practice as established for British officers? It could have resided in gaining and defending STATURE, especially from the model element of Power, the tactical ability in this case to win against his adversary. However, his resistance would not be possible without strengths stemming from SUBSTANCE.

In considering SUBSTANCE, I believe Guinness's character drew his courage from Standards, the level of performance that is acceptable by him based on his beliefs. Standards that were ingrained as an army officer and reinforced by his personality and identification of who he is, that is, of Person. His standard of conduct was simply to do everything by the book, and if so, he had performed according to Responsibilities and Practice of JOB.   This would explain his reliance on the authoritative and legal word of the Geneva Convention as a code as written.

The scene also reveals character traits of plain stubbornness and impractical idealism. He did not recognize, or care to acknowledge, that he moved into the region of CHALLENGE. He possesses Capabilities as a soldier and officer by the tradition and training, but by moving outside routine of JOB and being in a never experienced before situation, his current Practice as an officer was not sufficient or suitable in this situation.

SUBSTANCE is related to the individual as a person, having a unique background and particular abilities, and within it carries all his or her knowledge, skills, and judgment. SUBSTANCE of an individual would exist even if the individual were never to have walked through the front door of an organization, and it would still exist when that individual walks out the door. However, going out the door the individual should have more SUBSTANCE from learning and growth than when they walked in.

ELEMENTS OF SUBSTANCE

- Standards
- Person
- Capabilities

To understand SUBSTANCE is to answer the question "what is she made of?" Opinions of individuals are associated with such phrases as "I like the cut of his jib" or "she is my kind of person." In stressful situations, under pressure, the true fiber of the man or woman is revealed. I once heard said that if one were to know what makes a man angry, one would know how big that man is.

SUBSTANCE describes the whole person from self-image to unique talents, from their broad knowledge to employable skills, and from what they believe is right to what they will accept from themselves and from others as a work product. SUBSTANCE would be all they have to offer, if they were to choose to make it available, especially in an organization. As prescribed by the Responsibilities of JOB, what they provide is small and restricted as compared to the larger reservoir of everything they are and have to offer.

Unlike STATURE of the individual where it is more of standing within the organization, SUBSTANCE is permanent and enduring, either innate or the ingrained product of personal development, whether inside or outside the organization. An individual can feel the energizing lift of SUBSTANCE, if they were self-confident, or the inhibiting weight, if they were self-conscious. Within the context of and links with the other components and elements of the model of leadership, the refined leader draws from and influences the Standards, Person, and Capabilities associated with an individual's SUBSTANCE.

Standards has a dual meaning, one has to do with expectations and consistency, and the other with the acceptable level of performance or quality of work. Its connection to MEANING is through Relationship.

Person is the whole person, which includes what is appropriately revealed at work and what is kept private from work. It includes personality, family life, hobbies, beliefs, religion, cultural background, talents, and every aspect that makes this individual unique.

Capabilities are the individual's complete universe of skills, knowledge, and judgment for doing. From this totality, only a few skills and a small amount of knowledge and judgment are typically tapped and used for an organization in the domain of JOB.

RECOGNIZING SUBSTANCE

The engineer or manager in a leadership role will come to know increasingly more about an individual for whom they are responsible. For seeing more than just the little that is visible requires piecing together clues as they present themselves through the individual's words and actions. In conversation, an individual may volunteer much about themselves, or they may not.

When you first meet an individual, the three elements of SUBSTANCE (Standards, Person, and Capabilities) are jam-packed with content unable to be seen. Some content is fully developed from the individual's past, and some nascent in a progressing state of development. You and the individual will draw upon this content. Standards and Capabilities of the individual must be identified that fit the needs of the organization and that are required for the potential success of the individual. You must distinguish the level of fit and influence the individual's development, where needed.

For example, the Standards of an individual with just a few years experience in industry may have developed as part of his internal standards the habit of checking that he thoroughly completes his tasks and delivers them on time, and yet has not internalized the trait as a compulsion of following up with others on tasks they agree to complete on which he depends. With respect to Capabilities, he may have excellent basic skills with the computer, but he does not have a working knowledge of a few key software applications required specifically for his position in the organization. He may be currently adding this job-related skill to his profile of Capabilities. If the individual were new to the organization, then most of Capabilities will need to be augmented to match Responsibilities of JOB, unless his previous position was identical.

The more content within the elements of Standards and Capabilities that resulted from much experience in past organizations and positions, the less new additions in the areas of those elements are needed. Some individuals can adapt quickly and are fast learners, a characteristic of Person, and may easily displace old expectations of themselves, self-image, and work skills with new ones. This is especially true when the new things to learn are valid in the eyes of the individual based on the individual's judgment and knowledge—here experience helps the individual know what is important to learn and past education makes current learning easier. So you can teach the *right* old dog new tricks better than the wrong *new* dog those same new tricks.

Innate conscientiousness

One character trait of Person associated with Standards and Capabilities is conscientiousness. When this trait is ingrained, it underlies the drive of the individual as a worker. Individuals with innate conscientiousness are internally driven, knowing no other way to behave. They complete tasks thoroughly and on time, continually checking that no mistakes were made and that nothing was forgotten, and they are always professional and work at a high level. Individuals with this trait usually make it a point to work well with people. A manager would have to press an individual on all these points, if it were not for an internal compulsion of the individual. As a leader, you can have confidence the individual with this characteristic is living up to externally imposed expectations by others from this impulse from within.

I look for an innate conscientiousness whenever I interview a candidate for a position. One way to discover whether the candidate is conscientious is to look to past accomplishments, such as the completion of protracted tasks or involved projects that could be considered tedious. Also, look for completion of advanced formal education that required persistence and hard work. Another is to ask what tasks the individual does not like to do, inside or outside work, but does anyway. Ask for details on how they drive themselves to do them, and why they do them. You can see from the answers whether the individual has an innate conscientiousness.

Willingness and drive to grow

Another character trait of Person is a drive to grow in all the elements of SUBSTANCE, or as a minimum, a willingness to grow when needed. Growth comes from learning, and for humans this process continues from birth to grave. If one stops learning, one stops growing as an individual—for some, they stop living.

A question for the leader when getting to understand an individual is this: to what level of ability can this individual learn? How far and how fast, and how comfortable is he or she in moving from routine of JOB and into the model elements of CHALLENGE? And would they enjoy the excitement? Could they emotionally and socially handle the forced growth?

This characteristic also can be exposed in an interview. What did they recently learn? What were the details of the lesson and the method or medium from which they learned? Why did they take the time and expend the energy to learn that particular knowledge, skill, or piece of wisdom? How did they gain in wisdom by this experience? Did this experience add to their ability to use sound judgment in making decisions?

With a willingness to grow, an individual takes constructive criticism well and does not stubbornly resist new ideas or techniques. In fact, they look for the better idea or way of doing. An engineer in a management role will not be frustrated trying to get a point across to one for whom they are responsible or have an interest in their performance when this is the case. With the drive to grow, the point may not even need to be made, they are way ahead of the manager.

When outside the routine of JOB, and well into the far reaches of CHALLENGE—testing the limits of Unexplored, dealing with the vagaries of Chance, and sailing on the winds of Creativity—a drive to grow in the individual is reflected in the technological changes and growth in the organization. In this way, the success of the whole of the company cannot be distinguished from the success of its teams, and the success of the teams from the success of the individuals. The ability of the organization to learn and change mirrors these same abilities in the individuals of that organization. New routines for new technology that go into new products require the trait of a willingness and a drive to grow.

Having more ability to offer

Helping the individual, and a team of individuals, tap into Capabilities and Person, their unique background, experience, and unused talent is the role of the refined leader. The potential synergy of all the combinations of the unused facets of the team's individuals could be remarkable. A leader encourages rich interaction between team members for the technical matters and problems at hand.

As if pulling an ace from your sleeve, you in the role of a leader look to make the connection of an individual with a new endeavor in CHALLENGE, mostly outside the individual's boundary of JOB. This connection is in the form of what an individual might be suited to do beyond what they are currently doing. This being not only on a technical basis, but on the basis of emotional maturity and on the ability to grow in the consequential areas. You usually see indications for this from their past and in the ease with which they can perform tasks in their current roles.

One of your principal goals of leading is to help the individuals for whom you are responsible in their growth to be able to take over your position. By this, you and the organization are assured having workers that are best in class, while assuring depth in the ranks for growth in the business.

ELEMENT: STANDARDS

Standards as an element of SUBSTANCE, a component of the leadership model, is most effective and best expressed when the source is from within the individual. When they have expectations of themselves from what they know of themselves, nothing is stronger in motivation. The stronger the character of Person and the most accomplished in Capabilities, the stronger the motivation to attain in their work a high level of performance and quality.

You as manager or leader must add external Standards to the individual's internal Standards to fit the needs of JOB and CHALLENGE. You may even have to modify existing internalized Standards that you judge are not to the benefit of the individual or the organization. You do this mainly through providing MEANING (Purpose and Relationship) and definition around JOB (Responsibilities,

Practice, and Capacity). Standards of and for an individual are then a blend of those being internal, instilled, and imposed.

A source of commitment

An external expectation or rule is only effective when it is accepted by the individual, and that will occur only when the individual sees the need. Humans are good at ignoring what others think is important and they do not. You never want Standards to be forced on the individual. When forced upon them, they will not have commitment; they may follow, but not whole-heartedly, and they will never lead. Just to get along, they will go through the motions. Commitment is always better than acquiescence to imposed requirements for generating initiative and independent action.

Adding to the content the individual has already attained in the three elements of SUBSTANCE (Standards, Person, and Capabilities) takes effort, and usually conscious effort requiring time and expense. The persistence needed in learning new knowledge or skills that is not of an enjoyable nature takes commitment. Working at being better at anything requires an individual to believe it is in their best interest. This forms the basis for Overarching Principle #13:

Overarching Principle #13:

*Self-improvement is not possible until
there is an acceptance of the need by the individual
and the adoption of a new internalized standard.*

When Standards are ingrained they become a proxy of external control. How the individual thinks and behaves is governed by their commitment to their beliefs about what it means to do a good job. It is in this way that the leader is indirectly in control and executes authority without personally demeaning reprimands. Just reminding the individual in a professional manner that they have not met agreed upon Standards, or their personal Standards, is often enough. It is a way for the leader to be demanding without being petty through micromanaging or using a command-and-control approach.

A check to inappropriateness

In addition to Standards being internalized expectations, agreed upon by the individual and the leader, they are a countervailing force to balance and oppose a tendency for inappropriate over-friendliness or favoritism resulting from Relationship. For example, say you have been co-workers with a person for ten years who became a close friend, but now you have been promoted to be that person's boss. You will need to lean on the Standards you established for all in your group to establish the agreed to expectations to which your friend must abide. This would form the basis on how the new relationship will work. Standards are crucial to assure that you can continue to be friends, however, you and the others reporting to you will know that when it comes to performance and opportunity, you are and will be consistent with all.

The element of Relationship in the model is kept appropriate by exchanging information on a level related to work and to Purpose, or immediate goals. If friendships outside of the work environment were to emerge with those you associate with in business, always remember what you do or say could affect your management or leadership role back at work. It is best to always maintain your basic professional demeanor in social situations. If you would not say it or do it in a work setting, then do not say it or do it outside of work.

ELEMENT: PERSON

The refined leadership element of Relationship is used to go beyond just seeing the individual as a fit for the requirements of JOB. Individuals are not produced from a cookie cutter for a position description. The utmost for you is to have a grasp on understanding the individual's Person—no appreciation of SUBSTANCE is possible without it. We already covered how Relationship helps you to know the individual, and what he or she cares about. From Relationship you also can assess their strengths and fears, learn about unique and exceptional talents, and understand the current reality they deal with outside of work. You will also learn about Standards an individual imposes on himself or herself.

When an engineer or manager looks at the individual, but sees that individual as nothing more than job-related skills, then either the individual is perfect for JOB, or not; and it becomes difficult to accept something in between or to imagine more contribution of that individual. You have to see unique potentialities in order to influence the individual to perform better within JOB or to create novel things in the realm of CHALLENGE. Something cannot come from nothing, and what now exists cannot be changed, unless the individual is viewed more than a specification for a position. You will not know at first the beneficial potential outcomes from exposing and nurturing the individual's background or talents, but they are there.

At the intersection of different technologies, sciences, or industries lies a weather front of rain, storms, or a general unsettledness. It is from this passing front that change occurs in a company or an industry. Within the model element of Person are the makings of analogies and insights from other disciplines and industries, from cultures and methods of other companies, and from technologies and applied sciences different from what is currently being used in JOB.

Using more of what an individual has to offer from Person creates the weather frontal boundary. This process of cross-fertilization not only works with the connections from professional background, but also with unique life experiences, different cultural heritage or language, and different world views. In addition to work-related Capabilities, you as leader have available the entire and unique Person when providing encouragement to an individual solving a knotty problem or advancing beyond the state-of-the-art.

Apply the dangerous ingredient of emotion

When an individual is stretching into the leadership model's realm of CHALLENGE, or when just executing the routine of JOB to exacting Standards, an individual is drawing on Person. Pulling from somewhere deep within, an individual finds what they need emotionally to keep from giving up when striving for difficult objectives. When faced with overwhelming difficulty, why not just walk away? Some do. You want the individuals for whom you are responsible as a leader to be the ones who do not. Those who continue in the face of difficulty reach down to find what they always found in their life when needed, especially in order to have arrived to where they are today. Know they have this inside, and you have to help them find their particular something deep down when you sense they need it.

You cannot ignore the emotions of the individual. Be advised, their mettle at any point in time is related to emotion at that point in time, and to the individual's temperament in general. In coming to know the person, you will see how they react emotionally under stress, and their base emotional demeanor when unstressed. The leader influences emotion for the individual through the model components of MEANING and STATURE. Your aim is to keep emotion highly charged, but always positive for the individual.

Although humans have different personalities, they are similar when it comes to the effect on emotions of MEANING and STATURE. If you are strong in providing MEANING and successful in building their STATURE, in general, you as leader will influence emotions to be positive for the individual. You never want to use negative emotions to try to motivate the individual or team.

Learn what motivates the individual

Individuals are different when it comes to how they motivate themselves to work. This motivation is closely connected to innate conscientiousness and the emotion they have always drew upon to get them through long and hard work. The self-starters, those with initiative, do not require you to induce in them motivation. With others, you will be an important part of their drive. Each individual requires a different approach by you to help in this area. Through the model element Relationship, and learning more about Person, you learn what most likely will motivate the individual. What is it that they care about? What from their background pushes them forward? What fears about the future spur them on? What personal goals are they moving toward? These are only a few questions you can ask yourself, and through the model element of Relationship, you can indirectly and subtlety obtain the answers.

Money is a motivating factor, but it is not the prime factor for engineers and related technical professionals. It is not so much that they are not aware of the need of money for life's expenses, but to be successful in performing their type of work, they use a higher kind of thinking and emotion that is incompatible with money as a driver. Keeping money in mind displaces other thought processes. Although the long-term potential reward of money does provide the reason for consciously putting more time and physical effort into finding a creative solution or a novel idea, it does not contribute to the details of doing, to finding idea flow, or to being in the zone.

So, it is not so much money that strongly motivates technical professionals. Instead, engineers find and maintain motivation from a higher purpose for their work, a sense of professional duty, and a meaningful relationship with others on their team. As with any individual, they have personal philosophies, religious and political beliefs, and perspectives on the world that form a basis for motivation.

Character is associated with the model element of Person in the model component of SUBSTANCE. Everything covered thus far concerning background, beliefs, and life experiences help form the individual's character. A strong character will allow an individual to stand by their beliefs despite any negative consequences. Someone of good character is helpful to others, constructive in relationships, and a good example for others to follow. You as leader must recognize strong and good character in the individuals for whom you are responsible.

An individual may have a personal sense of destiny—the feeling that one is preparing for that one future moment of greatness. This can be another source of self-motivation in their work. As with all else within the model element of Person, be aware of the individual's aspirations and feelings of the future.

ELEMENT: CAPABILITIES

The overall knowledge from education, skills from training, and judgment from experience of an individual is greater than what is needed to match Responsibilities of JOB. Closely linked to Person and Standards, Capabilities stand alone in the customary matching of people with jobs. Obviously when it is said the candidate being considered for an open position is a good fit, it is referring to past employment background from which knowledge and skills are tied. Judgment is not so obvious a requirement for suitability for a position with a company, and it is hard to determination during the interviewing process, except by implication with past successes. It is a rare interviewer who can delve and discern a candidates possession of good judgment. Nevertheless, filling a position is matching the specific knowledge and skills specified for the position. The probability is then good the individual will contribute successfully to the routine efforts in JOB in supporting the operation of the business.

What of the excess knowledge and skills of Capabilities of the individual? They are available and needed for the basis of the individual's endeavors beyond JOB, in their confrontation with and growth from CHALLENGE. You will know of the individual's extra abilities from the model element Relationship, helping the relevance of these extra abilities be known by others, and influencing their use. As with all regarding SUBSTANCE, the individual has depth more than required for the specific tasks that make up their work in JOB.

Interview for more than specific knowledge and skills

Earlier in this chapter, I set the tone on how to interview for the strongest person for a position, although he or she may not be the best fit to the specification. If you were to hire on the matching of the individual's knowledge and skills as indicated by past employment to that in the requirements of the position, you may not be hiring an individual big enough for change and innovation. Interview for the whole of the individual's SUBSTANCE in terms of the leadership model. Although a CHALLENGE may not be identified for this individual at the moment, you can be assured this individual has well rounded and latent abilities with which to staff a project.

While you are determining the candidates innate conscientiousness during the interviewing process, as covered earlier in this chapter, you can explore the boundaries of all of the candidates technical and non-technical Capabilities. Be creative with your questions and apply a good dose of open-mindedness. Staffing for creation and growth, change and innovation, learning and success will require individuals that are more than just suited to carry on business as usual.

See in terms of strength

Here is a thought experiment: think of a successful, and well thought of, individual in your organization who may have had circumstances and good fortune help with that success. Now ask yourself, does this individual have weaknesses related or unrelated to the work? I would be surprised if you could not find any weaknesses. Now think of an unsuccessful, and *not* so well thought of, individual in your organization who may have had circumstances and bad fortune help with failures. Now ask yourself, does this individual have strengths related or unrelated to the work? I would be surprised if you could not find any strengths.

The perception of an individual's deficiencies are usually reinforced when others dwell on these weaknesses through gossip and outright criticism. When this takes on a surreptitious political nature, it is *poisoning the well* for that individual. The individual is then viewed as not being able to do anything right. Mistakes and inadequacies are harped upon and amplified beyond any valid level. Hearing the negative talk, the perception of this individual in most people's eyes is diminished, and nothing that individual can do will change the negative perception.

Even a manager may unconsciously see only the weaknesses of an individual for whom he or she is responsible. This is a case of the manager seeing the individual superficially and the results simplistically, never finding understanding below the surface. For a refined leader, nothing other than his or her own first-hand understanding should affect their judgment of an individual.

Think of the detrimental effect on the organization as a whole if zeroing in on weaknesses of individuals were the norm? I can assure you an environment of positive emotion would never exist. The following overarching principle is appropriate:

Overarching Principle #14:

No person, group, or team will ever appear good enough until there is a bias in perception toward strengths.

You must always manage to the strengths of those for whom you are responsible and strive to mitigate the effects of their weaknesses. Everyone has weakness, and these weaknesses can be identified with very little effort. Do not dwell on weaknesses; nothing comes of it but a nasty climate; just be concerned with building on an individual's strengths. The following quote by Peter Drucker, from his book *The Effective Executive*, expresses this idea nicely:

> Effective executives never ask "How does he get along with me?" Their question is "What does he contribute?" Their question is never "What can a man not do?" Their question is always "What can he do uncommonly well?"[3]

You, as leader, must make connections of what is useful from the whole of an individual's SUBSTANCE for their contribution to the success of the organization or the business. Those connections are easiest when made through Capabilities, especially when associated with the Responsibilities of JOB. Making connections of the useful-ness of strengths also applies to whether the individual is suitable for a particular foray into CHALLENGE, and in determining the depth into that region of the model that will not be overwhelming for the indi-vidual. These connections, and moving the reference points of knowledge, skills, and judgment, for an individual are the best way to come to know their potential.

Overarching Principle #13 complements Overarching Principle #14, and is the avenue for improvement in the areas where an indi-vidual is weak and strength is needed. You must help the individual accept the need for improvement. This may be the hardest task with some who are less than objective in seeing themselves, or less than honest with themselves. Seeing the need may be easier for them once they are faced with the difficulties stemming from extended Responsibilities of JOB or non-routine tasks of CHALLENGE. Do not forget to tap the whole of SUBSTANCE to aid in the continuous im-provement of an individual's Capabilities. The expectations they have of themselves within Standards and the motivating factors found deep within Person can only help drive them in learning.

CHAPTER *7*

JOB AND ORGANIZATIONAL KNOW-HOW

"Every advance begins in a small way and with the individual. The mass can be no better than the sum of the individuals. Advancement begins within the man himself; when he advances from half-interest to strength of purpose; when he advances from hesitancy to decisive directness; when he advances from imma-turity to maturity of judgment..."

Henry Ford, My Life and Work (Autobiography)[1]

Faced with repeat failures of a control component on a boiler we manufactured where I once worked, personnel representing the quality and manufacturing functions and I, representing engineering, were not sure whether it was a design issue or a supplier issue. We were perplexed for days trying to find the root cause of the failures. We struggled because no one involved was the right individual for this type of control work. I was then able to turn to our electrical control engineer who just returned from being out of the office on business. I had confidence he could solve the problem easily. This confidence stemmed from understanding the model of leadership component of SUBSTANCE for him, especially work-related knowledge, skills, and judgment found in the model element Capabilities. In short, he was qualified to do the work. After a few day's at various boiler units in our engineering lab, he called me over. Using a few screens of his oscilloscope, he interpreted voltages and currents displayed as various sine waves and horizontal lines with distortions, jumps, and dips. I understood his analysis as he explained it, and agreed on his proposed cause of the problem and on his solution because it made sense. The cause of the failures of the control component was then easily eliminated in the manufactured product.

The point of this story is with the right person even the most difficult work is simply a matter of giving it attention for completion in due course. When Capabilities of SUBSTANCE of the individual provide the specific work-related knowledge, skills, and judgment required of Responsibilities and Practice in the leadership model component of JOB, it is a matter of routine. In the area of JOB, outcomes are expected with little uncertainty, and they carry little risk. Unknowns are minimal with work that has been performed many times before. Whenever possible, assign the right person for the work in JOB, and it will appear to be easy and routine.

As an example, an architect designing her one hundredth house is at the level of professional practice that she is confident any new surprises will be minor in nature; it has become routine for her. That was not always the case, and with the first few she designed she needed to grow her Capabilities to meet her Responsibilities of her new professional offering as designer of houses. And to illustrate the difference between JOB and CHALLENGE, with these first few house designs she was in the realm of CHALLENGE, maybe not for moving the industry or profession to new advances, but for her as an individual adding to her responsibility-related Capabilities, Practice and Capacity within JOB.

Another point to get out of the opening story in this chapter is about solving problems and the nature of know-how. If any problem is to be solved, then it must be understood by seeing the moving parts. Before the electrical control engineer became involved, the others and I were seeing only the superficial mechanical aspects of the control component. It was not within our ken to even know what to observe, let alone interpret what we would have observed. Seeing the moving parts of the situation as the control engineer did with the oscilloscope requires knowing what moving parts one is looking for, then observing and interpreting. This is related to know-how. The right individual with the right Capabilities makes the work of JOB routine, sees the moving parts of otherwise obscure situations, and provides the medium within which know-how resides.

As a side note, the refined leadership model gives you a method to see the moving parts of leading individuals and teams. It provides a framework by which your observations, fact gathering, and issues with people fit together as moving parts. Even though the model is a snapshot in time of the state of leading one individual, it is fluid, and constantly changing. It is to help *you* be the right person for the work of leading, and making this difficult work routine.

THE RECTANGLE IN THE CENTER

In order for you to be able to inspire an individual to go beyond which he or she is currently accountable, or to delegate with confidence a task or undertaking, you as manager or leader must know the individual is technically qualified or close to being qualified. Is the individual technically competent to perform the work of current Responsibilities of JOB? If so, then they are ready to grow further, or lead in the leadership model component of CHALLENGE for change or innovation. To create meaningful change and to create new products or technology in an organization or an industry, the individual should be able to perform the basics of the related customary work, which could be used as a footing from which to step toward innovation. When I was interviewing for my first position out of engineering school, I wanted to go directly into R&D. One interviewing manager said that I would only be ready for that kind of role after I had acquired experience with the product, technology, and market that I would be changing. At the time, I disagreed, but now I have to say he was right.

The rectangle in the center of the model of leadership signifies the boundary of JOB, and it can be small or large in relation to the other symbolic rectangles of MEANING, SUBSTANCE, STATURE, and most significantly to that of CHALLENGE. Some position descriptions encompass more of CHALLENGE with a larger JOB rectangle, such as R&D, engineering, and corporate change agents; they still have routine in JOB, but now more of the elements of CHALLENGE are part of the routine, such as Unexplored, Chance, and Creativity.

To assign an individual to a task or project beyond their current duties is to ask them to move beyond the rectangle of JOB into CHALLENGE, outside of the world of their day-to-day activities. More risk and uncertainty is involved, and they define as part of CHALLENGE what is expected of them and of their team. A larger portion of someone's activities when entering the realm of CHALLENGE involves more of themselves from what is associated with SUBSTANCE and STATURE. In supporting them in this, you must do more leading, and less managing, which means being less firm in the expectations of end results.

Competence at JOB *is paramount*

The individual must perform competently in JOB. Reliability and safety of bridges, elevators, airplanes, buildings, washing machines, cell phones, and everything we use start with individuals knowing what they are doing. If an individual for whom you are responsible is less than competent, then you must ensure that they receive the proper training and have expert supervision until they are. It is all right to have beginning or intermediate practitioners in a profession or a company, but it is not all right to allow them to practice in critical areas without them knowing their limitations. Learning and self-improvement in Standards and Capabilities of the individual was covered in the previous chapter, and Overarching Principle #13 applies here.

The daily operation of an organization or company provides the revenue and income from which it survives and grows. Without the competency of many individuals satisfying the needs of customers through execution, and without the monetizing of know-how and core technologies by these many individuals, there would be no business. This all resides in the routine of JOB.

Defining competency, and identifying who is competent, is sometimes less than straightforward. The statement "Either he can fly a jet airliner or he cannot" may be too simple. What are the boundaries within which flying a jet airliner is routine for him, and as you approach the boundaries of his competencies, how much do the attendant risks and uncertainties go up? If he spent his early years flying combat missions off an aircraft carrier, or flying into the eye of hurricanes, then the conditions he may see as a commercial airline pilot will rarely move him beyond his limits of competency. He might never move beyond routine of JOB, and into the risk and uncertainty of CHALLENGE.

The degree of competency of the individuals for whom you are responsible will make or break you as a manager. You will either succeed when they do, and look good, or not succeed when they do not, and look bad. However, the goal is not how their competency makes you look in the eyes of others. The goal is to hold up your end of Responsibilities of *your* JOB within the company. Matching an individual's assigned tasks and projects, the model element of Responsibilities, to their level of competency is your role as a manager; influencing their growth through training and the right doses of CHALLENGE is your role as a leader. The ideas and principles of refined leadership, and the model of leadership, give you the tools to do this.

Jumping off point into Unexplored

The probability of success, and the probable level of accomplishment of that success, is increased by starting with know-how as close as possible to the CHALLENGE goal. This know-how should be demonstrated in the form of routine of JOB. As an example, assume you are responsible for penetrating a distinctly new market for one of your company's products. You have two possible individuals with the following know-how as alternatives for assigning as product manager to lead a team. The first is expert on the product and current markets, but knows nothing of the new market. The second knows nothing of the product or current markets, but is expert from routine of his work on the new market. By the suggestion above, the closest you can get with existing know-how is the second alternative. The second alternative person has no existing know-how of the existing products, but others do within the organization, and are available for his team. The Unexplored, Chance, and Creativity of CHALLENGE is that of the new market. The individual who is the second alternative is closest to the objective of the change. There is a foundation from JOB from which to start.

CHALLENGE absorbs more unpredictable time and stressful energy from the individual than the routine of JOB. Relatedness becomes a big factor to what degree an individual or team finds difficulty with non-routine tasks. The closer the goals of a project for change or creating something new with established processes and existing organization, the less stress on the existing routines and people, as well as less risk and uncertainty. Jumping off points for change and innovation are better from strength, or from what you understand best, and with individuals of known Capabilities. This revolves around JOB.

ELEMENTS OF JOB

- Responsibilities
- Practice
- Capacity

JOB, a component of the refined leadership model, is the central piece from which MEANING, SUBSTANCE, STATURE, and CHALLENGE are tied. The element of Capabilities is part of SUBSTANCE of the individual, but it overlaps into JOB with the knowledge, skills, and judgment that correspond to and satisfy Responsibilities of JOB. See Figure 7.1, *JOB Overlaps SUBSTANCE Around Capabilities*.

The elements of JOB are compatible with an analytical approach to managing, what I have been calling *managing only*. Responsibilities, Practice, and Capacity are what would be left if you were to strip away the nebulous nature of leading people. In JOB, issues could be easily made black and white through objectivity,

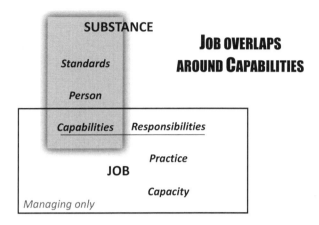

Fig. 7.1   JOB Overlaps SUBSTANCE Around Capabilities.
Capabilities part of SUBSTANCE of the individual, but it overlaps
into Job with the knowledge, skills, and judgment

where rationality governs over emotion. Elements of JOB are necessary, but not sufficient when moving into CHALLENGE, when leading individuals in the areas of creation and growth for change and innovation.

ELEMENT: RESPONSIBILITIES

The element of Responsibilities is the tasks and functions for which the individual is accountable to the organization, and are formalized by the traditional position description for a given position. These items may be listed in the formal position description using statements such as "Responsible for providing application engineering calculations to sales engineers in support of preparation of sales proposals, 15%", or "Responsible for traveling to construction sites as needed to supervise the installation of company's products, 5%".

These tasks are of standard procedures and are routine in conducting the business of the company.

The model element of Responsibilities is associated with JOB and not with CHALLENGE. Responsibilities in the realm of CHALLENGE are in the form of objectives being worked toward, are non-routine, and are new to or additional for the individual; they may eventually become Responsibilities of JOB.

It has been explained that the knowledge, skills, and judgment required to be successful in meeting Responsibilities in a given position is a subset, or a small part of the total Capabilities of the individual. For the individual to grow to be competent for more or higher level Responsibilities, the individual must leave the comfort of routine and venture into the area of CHALLENGE to acquire new abilities that are at least new to the individual, if not the company. For practical application ideas for Responsibilities, see the section in Chapter 9, entitled *Capabilities-Responsibilities Interface.*

ELEMENT: PRACTICE

Practice is how work is carried out. It is adhering to standard processes, methodologies, rules, and guidelines. It includes conforming to industry codes and standards, and also conforming to laws and regulations. For learned professionals, it is also conformance to the customary practices of that profession.

In industry, there is a traditional consistency of Practice between ways of doing things for individuals of the same type of work or department. For example, welders of natural gas pipelines across different service organizations will have similar work procedures, or project engineers constructing municipal roads will have similar working routines across different engineering firms or municipalities. Within a given organization, department, or group, processes can range from being customary and unwritten to being formalize with prescribed steps on how to precisely perform work. Some are specific to a company, while others are industry-wide or part of a profession.

When in the realm of CHALLENGE, it may become necessary to disregard certain points of Practice or to even break rules. Change and innovation require new routines and standard procedures, and to arrive at this new Practice, a transient condition must exist between the current and the new. For practical application ideas for Practice, see the section in Chapter 9, entitled *Practice-Power Interface.*

ELEMENT: CAPACITY

Capacity is the volume of work an individual is able to complete with respect to Capabilities and Practice. It includes the individual's ability to perform a given quantity of work at a given speed and the ability to maintain focus. Capacity includes the output obtained through persistence, working hard, and effectiveness by working smart. It is the ability to do more without sacrificing expectations or acceptable levels of quality of Standards and Practice.

Any individual has a given level of ability to accomplish work in a given time, that is, the quantity of results at the required quality level in relation to time. It is not enough that he or she has the requisite knowledge and skills, or follows Practice. The individual must possess the faculty to focus and persevere, to maintain attention, and not get sidetracked, until tasks and projects are completed.

The model element of Capacity is crucial for accelerated timing, or when the amount to be accomplished is large in relation to the number of available individuals. Capacity has two shades to its meaning: one for the individual's ability, and the other for a group's combined abilities with respect to quantity of work. For the individual, it is a matter of mastery of knowledge and skills, and their effective application through good judgment. For a group or team, it is a matter of headcount and the degree of complementary Capabilities of the individual members. You, as leader, can influence Capacity with regard to both shades of meaning through the use of teams.

BUILDING A TEAM, GROUP, OR DEPARTMENT

An individual is the base unit of agency, that is an entity with conscious thought and deliberate action to achieve a goal. A team of two individuals is the next level of such agency. A two person team is known as a dyad. When the two team members are compatible and complementary in SUBSTANCE, JOB and STATURE, and when they compare favorably in Purpose, the resulting outcomes from better effectiveness are greater than double. I have experienced firsthand the positive effects of this type of team as a team member.

The next level up on the teaming scale is not surprisingly composed of three individuals. As with two, the resulting effectiveness when they perform as a true team, that is, not just as a group of three individuals with no synergistic influence on each other, is greater than triple. It depends on the actual individuals and team, but on the high end I estimate the multiple could be in double digits.

Ultimately, a team can be made up of more than three individuals. Depending on the team leadership's strength and their understanding of team mechanics, an optimum size is reached before effectiveness as a team starts to drop off with no further benefit obtained by adding to the number of members.

Useful to organizations is the cross-functional, or multi-functional, team. It is composed of individuals, each representing a functional perspective that should have a contribution in the results. For example, if developing a product, the team should have an individual from engineering, manufacturing, marketing, sales, accounting, quality, field/customer service, and a user. The use of a cross-functional team is best when pursuing a goal in the model component of CHALLENGE. Overarching Principle #15 follows:

Overarching Principle #15:

*No probability of success is high until there is
an appropriate set of individuals, with the right capabilities,
accepting the challenge as a true team.*

Just throwing people together does not guarantee success. There has been much research on teams and much has been written about them. If you have not already, I suggest you read a few books on teaming. I will not go into detail on the subject of teams, other than how you can use the refined leadership model to select individuals for a team. Also, the ideas and principles in this book are directly applicable to interacting with individuals on the team, and leading the team as a whole.

When putting together a team, you must come to understand each individual from the perspective of their snapshot of the model of leadership. Figure 7.2, *Teams and Projects Move an Organization*, shows where the refined leadership model components and elements fit in with team projects when bringing about change to existing processes, technologies, products, and markets.

First, look to connect at their Capabilities: work-related knowledge, skills, and judgment. You want the team members to have the

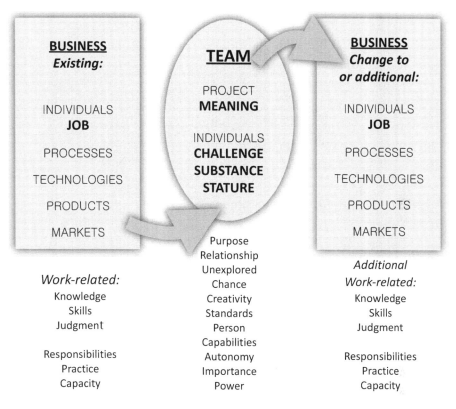

Fig. 7.2 Teams and Projects Move an Organization. Effective and least disruptive for creation or change, requires separation of individuals from their daily duties of business operation; shows parts and elements of leadership model.

right Capabilities for the projected work, and as close as possible to the new knowledge, skills, and judgment related to the change. This is the idea as presented in the previous section, *Jumping off point into Unexplored.* Overall, you are adding individual models in the area of responsibility-related Capabilities associated with JOB. This gives the team a composite Capabilities. The group as a true team can now jump off into the realm of CHALLENGE with competencies closely related to the ultimate goal, and with an increased level of the model element of Capacity.

Second, look to the model element of Purpose. The immediate goal of the project must be shared by members as a mutual commitment, and it must be compatible with higher level Purpose of each individual separately in the organization. For example, say there are two individuals on a team who both share the immediate goal of finding the best way of modifying a product to urgently solve a defect problem. The first individual from purchasing has an additional higher Purpose with respect to JOB of lowering cost of procured components. The other team member from engineering has an additional higher Purpose with respect to JOB of revising the product to function closer to the user's need. Since they do not share a higher Purpose, there may be a less than positive outcome for the team.

Third, look to Standards and Person of each individual. This will give you an estimation of the potential interactions and dynamics of the team. These elements of SUBSTANCE for each individual do not have to be similar, but they must be workably consistent, or reconcilable, otherwise you may see team member compatibility problems. For example, say the Standards for one individual is such that she will not stop working on a task until she feels satisfied it is as perfect as she feels it should be. Her decisions are all driven by test data. Her teammate's internal Standards compel him to go just so far until he feels it is good enough, then stopping, letting it sit while he starts or moves on to another task. His decisions are based on analysis and logic, supported by little data. No one way is correct, only what is suitable for a given situation. Unless the personality and temperament of Person allows each to see how this difference can make them stronger together as a team, there will be compatibility issues on the team and no synergy of interaction.

Lastly, look to the model elements of Autonomy, Importance, and Power that form the STATURE of each individual on the team. STATURE matters more for success in the realm of CHALLENGE than in JOB. In the unstructured world of striving for objectives that have never been achieved before or of solving problems that have no current solutions, the individuals driving the change will need to step beyond boundaries when it comes to obtaining resources and dealing with established organizational procedures and rules. They will have to overcome many obstacles of inertia; STATURE moves an organization, not a right answer or a good solution. In addition, a mismatch in STATURE of team members may allow some to pull rank or try to unduly influence the team as a result of their formal authority or higher status in the organization. The principles and lessons of refined leadership must be followed within the team setting to forestall the bad situations that could arise from a mismatch and misuse of STATURE by any individual as a member of that team.

As a leader outside the team, you should interact with the team in the same way you would an individual using refined leadership methods. The team will eventually start acting as one entity, but it is still composed of individuals, and the individual is still the base unit of Relationship and for providing MEANING. If you are the team leader as a member of the team, just use refined leadership and the model as you would in any other leadership situation.

CORE TECHNOLOGIES AND THE FIRM

Consider a bakery and assume they make the best bread around. In order to provide a living for the owner and employees, this bakery must sell many loaves every day, and each loaf must be of the same differentiating goodness for customers to keep coming back. They do this through implementation of the bakery's core technologies, or put another way, through each individual doing what they know how to do as a routine for this purpose, and aided by tools and machines refined by them. They may apply a few trade secrets to obtain their good results. There was a time when this was not routine, but experimental until they learned. What is more, the routine nature of applying knowledge and skills in producing a product gives them the opportunity to continually improve the core technologies and know-how of providing a product. For this bakery, as is the case with any organization, know-how and core technologies reside with individuals in the component of the model of leadership of JOB.

A core technology of a company is not one being developed, but one that is already expressed in the company's current products. For new technologies to be useful and monetized, they must express themselves in the marketplace through a product or service. This can only be possible by being imbedded in JOB of many individuals who are all working toward a common end; they became the creation of new routine. Outcomes from CHALLENGE are the basis of new routine, adding to or replacing existing Capabilities, Responsibilities, Practice, and Capacity. This leads to the next overarching principle:

Overarching Principle #16:

Know-how and technology are tacit and informal, residing in the heads of individuals. Yet when formalized, both still need to be in the heads of those effectively using them; it becomes their craft.

My first manager of engineering position was with a company that moved from one part of the country to another. I was new to the company. I was hired to create a new engineering group at the new location. The engineering personnel were all new, none of the engineering employees from the old location made the move. All the engineering filing cabinets were moved from the old to the new location. They contained letters, memos, reports, drawings, bill of materials, procedures, sketches, and notes. I guess we had as much as anyone would want in the way of formal, written knowledge concerning the company's products and core technologies.

During the interviewing process I asked about the potential problems that would be faced by having lost the experienced engineers, design drafters, and technicians. "No problem," I was told, "all the files and drawings have been moved and are available to you". I took the position and in time I learned much about the nature of know-how—this became another Galapagos Islands for me by way of extremes in isolating for me another phenomenon in technical management.

Supporting the business with this formal codified knowledge alone was not easy; no individuals were familiar enough with the knowledge or possessed the pertinent concrete skills. With customers calling with problems, manufacturing needing answers, sales orders being executed, and application engineering supporting critical future sales, not enough time or surplus energy were available to me and the new engineering personnel to go over, digest, understand, and use correctly, effectively, or efficiently what was in those filing cabinets.

The technologies were in the heads of those who did not make the move with the company. These were many of the same people who had created the know-how in the first place, and who came to use it routinely. The composite know-how required to operate at high levels was not yet in the heads of the new individuals, and the application of core technologies was not yet routine, or part of the individual's craft or skills. They could not see yet the moving parts.

Degree to which know-how is embedded in organization

Although new know-how and technology are created in the leadership model component of CHALLENGE, the *what* of know-how will ultimately be part of Responsibilities, Practice and Capacity of JOB and reside in the responsibilities-related knowledge, skills, and judgment of Capabilities in the SUBSTANCE of individuals.   The *where* of the *application* of know-how as situated in the organization in relation to the customer and the *when* of its *application* in time relation to the sale or use of the product or service determines how deeply the know-how and technologies are imbedded in the organization. The further from the customer the know-how is implemented into a product or service with respect to *where* and *when* in the value chain, then...

1. the more deeply know-how and technology are fixed within the organization,
2. the more leveraged the return on the investment, and
3. the more the uncertainty and the greater the consequences from risk.

The following illustrates this by comparing two situations. One is a manufacturing company with a standard product, such as a refrigerator, and the other is an engineering firm with a design service, such as custom air conditioning (AC) system design for buildings. The refrigerator in the manufacturing environment is designed and developed at a distance from the ultimate customer and user. In contrast, the custom AC system design has direct client involvement in its design, designed specifically for the client. (The more customized the product in the manufacturing company to a specific customer specification, the more this situation approaches the engineering design firm.)

In the manufactured standard product case, the refrigerator, a team develops and validates in the realm of CHALLENGE a new product and associated organizational processes using the best information available on satisfying a target customer, or market segment. Included in the development are the processes by which the organization will add value with each step of manufacture for each unit produced. The final results of their efforts are formal documentation and procedures to be used in the mass manufacture from hundreds to millions of units of this standard product for a number of years. Know-how and technology expressed in this product become embedded in processes, production equipment, and facilities. Many individuals in the organization will find new routine in JOB associated with this new standard product, combining all the newly acquired know-how represented by responsibility-related knowledge, skills, and judgment.

The case for the design engineering firm offering custom AC system design for buildings is quite different. A project team applies the practice of their profession to the requirements and specification of one client. The know-how used is connected to JOB, not CHALLENGE—unless new know-how or technology is needed for that particular project. Individual professionals apply knowledge, skills, and judgment applicable for their profession, say in mechanical engineering. It is the routine of applying the same know-how as on prior projects, but now applied to the current client specification. The routine for designing customized systems is built into the professional's model component of JOB. This brings the implementation of know-how closer to the customer and use than in the case of the refrigerator. If new know-how or technology is learned, it can be codified into the organizations processes and procedures, but much is retained with project team individuals as tacit knowledge. To the degree each individual maintains that particular know-how, it might be an example of use it or loose it. Know-how is with the practicing professionals and with their client relationships. It is less imbedded within the organization than that associated with the manufacture of a refrigerator.

The location of where new know-how is embedded has implications for where the focus of refined leadership is required for the greatest entrepreneurial impact. For the manufacturer of a standard product, such as the refrigerator, it is in the area of CHALLENGE, with Unexplored, Chance, and Creativity. For the engineering design firm, in our example designing custom AC systems for buildings, the focus with the greatest entrepreneurial impact is in the model component of JOB, with Responsibilities, Practice, Capacity, and related Capabilities of individuals.

You cannot expect an organization with a dominant orientation of our first case of the standard product to be able to function well as an organization providing custom designed products or services, and the custom design firm cannot function as a mass producer. The flexibility to make this switch on the fly is rarely built into the structure of an organization; it would take major change in the organization through effort in the area of CHALLENGE.

Growth requires know-how to be scalable

As stated previously, change and innovation, plus the creation of new know-how and technology, are best brought about by a team operating in the leadership model component of CHALLENGE. The results will require the new know-how to reside in the responsibilities-related knowledge, skills, and judgment of the individual in future JOB. If the growth of the business were involved and a new product or service resulted in an appreciably different know-how and technology base, then it would require the establishment of

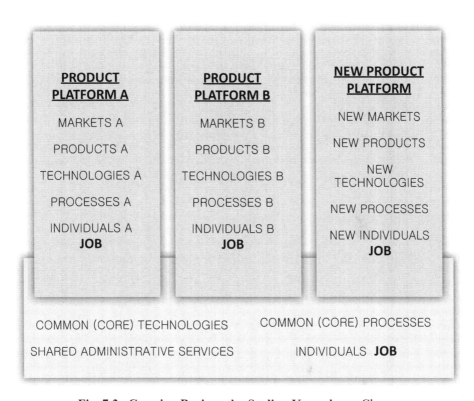

Fig. 7.3 Growing Business by Scaling Know-how. Change
and innovation requires separate cognizance in new knowledge,
skills, and judgment for each platform added.

a set of new individuals in area of JOB, supporting new processes
and new markets.   This is graphically illustrated with Figure 7.3,
Growing Business by Scaling Know-how. Scaling up requires a way
to keep adding responsibility-related Capabilities in the organization
at a working level without diminishing the Capacity or competency
in providing to the customer existing and new products and services.
The right box of Figure 7.2 (p.169) with the label *Business /
Changed To or Additional* corresponds to the right box of Figure 7.3

with the label *New Product Platform*, which could have been labeled *New Service*, or *New Value Stream*.

I have seen the mistake smaller companies make as a result of their limited resources. Its the same for companies that have many diverse product lines from years past, developed by individuals no longer with the company, and requiring much daily attention to detail in support of the operation of the business. These companies constrain their ability to be more competitive by not scaling their resources properly. They pile onto the same individuals new Responsibilities, Practice, and Capacity of new JOB onto existing JOB; and this on top of previous existing JOBS. In this case, individuals cannot dedicate the necessary portion of their time and energy to any one area of know-how and core technology. No time or desire is left to develop the necessary perspective that crosses functional boundaries within the organization, or that senses the marketplace and the competitive situation. Their daily activities required to support many diverse product lines do not allow adequate cognizance of innumerable detail, nor does it permit decisions based on awareness of history and current happenings surrounding everything about the product or service. You cannot base growth of the business on spreading individuals thin.

Which comes first, business growth or additional resources? Many who run companies finesse growth by balancing return from a new product or service with adding the expense of more individuals. This question of what comes first, the chicken or the egg, is one reason growth through development of new products and services is difficult for many companies. I say additional resources come first because a new product or service is a financial investment in growth that will provide a return in time, similar to any financial investment.

CHAPTER 8

STATURE OF THE INDIVIDUAL

"... I always go to sea as a sailor, because of the wholesome exercise and pure air of the forecastle deck. For as in this world, head winds are far more prevalent than winds from astern..., so for the most part the Commodore on the quarter-deck gets his atmosphere at second hand from the sailors on the forecastle. He thinks he breathes it first; but not so. In much the same way do the commonalty lead their leaders in many other things, at the same time that the leaders little suspect it."

Ishmael's narration,
Herman Melville, Moby-Dick[1]

Within this component of the refined leadership model lies the means to influence the exercise of the full strength of each individual for whom you are responsible. Here is where you inspire change for the positive in the individual's self image and in how others view them. It is this component of the model where you provide the freedom for the individual to offer more of themselves, so personal fiber fully expresses itself. And here is where an individual, venturing into CHALLENGE, has the wherewithal to maneuver and to pull off a win for the organization.

I have written that you as a leader should not only believe in yourself, but in others. This belief stems from confidence in what can be found in SUBSTANCE of an individual compared to the potential STATURE of that individual. By positively influencing STATURE, you will allow the best in an individual to come out, thus obtaining the full effect of SUBSTANCE. Where SUBSTANCE is currently of higher level than STATURE, the individual will surprise those in the organization by being so much better in action than any thought possible. Elevating the STATURE by offering objectives in the area of CHALLENGE in this case corrects a situation where the individual could easily become bored, or feel trapped in a dead-end job. On the other hand, without an individual having fairly good levels for SUBSTANCE and JOB, elevating STATURE too far too fast could result in disappointing and undesirable performance, both in appearance and reality. In this case, the words and actions of an individual who has been given or has taken too much in the way of Autonomy, Importance, and Power at the extreme will show itself as an individual exhibiting poor understanding and judgment, having difficulty working with people, possibly displaying self-importance and shallow puffery, and in general, as they say, appearing to be all show, no go. Strengths and weaknesses become apparent as individuals are put in the situation of more or less forcing their growth in STATURE.

Change and innovation from an organization require more individuals successfully flexing into the area of CHALLENGE beyond the confines of JOB. An organization with a disproportionate amount of focus on routine of JOB, and one that comfortably performs continuous improvement for only operational perfection, will tend to neglect expending creative energy on entrepreneurial change. By bringing routine into better balance with venturing into the elements of Unexplored, Chance, and Creativity, you encourage individuals out of this efficiency trap. To do this, individuals will need to be better armed with the necessary levels of STATURE. A good source of cultural energy for change and innovation in an organization, and a way to unlock the potential from its collective SUBSTANCE, is to build up the STATURE of many individuals as members of teams.

Unlike SUBSTANCE of the individual, STATURE is less permanent and enduring. Instead of the elements of STATURE being innate or the ingrained product of personal development as they are with SUBSTANCE, it is more of standing within the organization, and reinforced by interaction with people. Although STATURE in general originates with an individual's positive attitude, it is his or her demeanor, actions, successes, and failures which form the perception in others confirming what the individual feels. Therefore, unlike SUBSTANCE of the individual, STATURE is neither secure nor portable. How many engineers, managers, or executives who once had great STATURE in a company, but despite the fact that their SUBSTANCE is the same, find themselves with reduced STATURE in a different position at a new company, or with no STATURE while looking for a job?

As an example, within a company in which I once worked, I witnessed firsthand how the engineering department went from being viewed as the strongest part of that business, and considered leaders in their industry, to being viewed as the worst part of that business, all in just one year. The department's STATURE changed. New owners and new key employees became active detractors. Those who promoted STATURE of that particular department in the past now were politically weakened themselves. It was the new owners and employees perception that changed, and not the SUBSTANCE or JOB of individuals, or the methods of the engineering department to address CHALLENGE.

Remember this always, for I have seen it over and over with many individuals and functional groups, STATURE is giveth, and STATURE is taketh away. It is given with good press and hype, or it is taken away with disinformation and the pushing of misconceptions. In this situation, Overarching Principle #14 is not only not followed, but the opposite can occur; no person, group, or team is good enough due to a politically biased perception of weakness.

ELEMENTS OF STATURE

Each of the following elements compose STATURE and are covered in detail in this chapter:

- Autonomy
- Importance
- Power

Those without STATURE are not heard, and their ideas or counsel are not sought and not considered. They can be invisible in the organization.

Attendant to a lack of STATURE is a lack of MEANING. A Relationship with a sense of Purpose, the two elements of MEANING, are the foundation for the individual desiring and attaining the appropriate level of STATURE within the organization. You as leader are responsible for providing the positive benefits of MEANING (see Chapter 4) in an effort to instill a desire in the individual for STATURE.

Autonomy is the freedom offered to an individual that is more than governed by Practice of JOB, which to various degrees is imposed by standard operating procedures, codes and regulations, formal and informal rules, policies in the personnel handbook, hierarchy of the command structure, and idiosyncrasies of a boss's authority. It includes the hours and place of work, and all other details and expectations related to conformity to norms in the organization.

Importance is the significance attached to the individual's work in connection with the business side of the organization, and to his or her feelings of importance. Individual initiative, self-confidence, accountability, and ownership of a task or project springs from Importance.

Power is the ability to gets things done and to achieve objectives, going outside the standard structure or procedures. Bending the rules as needed falls under this element of the refined leadership model, as do tactics and strategy, game theory and playing to win.

IT'S RELATIVE, FORMAL AND ASSUMED

The Stature of an individual is relative. One person acts with more authority on matters than another, even though the other may have more formal authority in the organization. Personality (from SUBSTANCE) is a big factor for how comfortable a given individual feels with their level of STATURE, and to what degree the elements of STATURE would be assumed in certain situations. Another big factor is your instilling the confidence in the individual to accept a new level of STATURE as needed in the context of a situation. This is when an individual *steps up*, as they say.

When STATURE is assumed informally, it becomes indistinguishable from formal authority by those interacting with the individual and accepting their higher STATURE. This is the case of the so called *natural leader*, especially if this tendency were to assume STATURE is coupled with a charismatic presence. To successfully assume STATURE at a given level, an individual will need to have the appropriate levels of talent and character from SUBSTANCE so others will see the individual as a convincing leader to follow.

VULNERABILITY OF A LEADER

In order for you to aid in the building of STATURE for individuals for whom you are responsible, each individual needs to take front stage while you stay in the background. With your support, you make known causally and formally the good results from their work, you encourage a higher visibility for them within the organization, and you publicly praise them. In short, where it is valid, you make them look good.

Building their STATURE in this way may have a downside effect, depending on the culture of the organization. *You* may appear weak, since it will appear to be the individuals reporting to you who know everything and do all the work. Not touting the part you played in the successes of your reports is what is meant by behind the scenes, and behind the scenes *is* behind the scenes. The perception is that you are not involved. But this is what is needed in order to help the individual develop independence and importance, lose their fear by feeling indispensable, and have optimism and confidence. This leads to Overarching Principle #17:

Overarching Principle #17:

As a leader, one grows stronger by allowing vulnerability; one will only seem weak by making others appear strong.

This is a tall order for an engineer-turned-manager who is used to directly performing the work hands-on. Remember what I stated in Chapter 1, that a common failing of engineer-turned-manager is the inability to let go of performing and controlling the technical work, and the inability to not treat his or her reports as extensions of himself or herself. Guard against conforming to the popular view of leader as the one in charge. Sometimes saying "I don't know" is the better response then to try to appear to know it all, and fail. Rely on those who are cognizant with their projects to know more than you since they are responsible, accountable, and qualified based on SUB-STANCE, JOB, and STATURE to do so. What you can be proud of, instead of your knowing it all, is your positive influence. You as one person cannot have greater abilities to achieve compared to the composite SUBSTANCE, JOB, and STATURE of those reporting to you. You alone are not scalable, but the potential of your team is.

If you take Overarching Principle #17 and state it in a reverse fashion, it would also be true: *as a leader, one grows weaker while trying to appear strong by making others appear weak.* In a fellowship as described early, those you help will know the contribution you make to everyone's success or failure; let your leadership speak for itself. And remember the concept that the manager or leader is responsible for all failure and the individual for all success.

ELEMENT: AUTONOMY

Individuals know themselves and know how they work best. One might be more productive in the morning on certain kinds of tasks, such as writing reports or physically using their hands, while being better at performing other tasks in the afternoon or late evening, such as planning or conceptualizing. Some work better in cubicles and offices, while others in conference rooms or on the road. Location and time of day are variables with infinite combinations that have an impact on the performance of the individual. This particularly applies to being creative and solving problems, or similar tasks requiring the functioning of the higher evolved reaches of the brain. It applies to anything needing to be accomplished or solved outside the physical world, usually by attaining a state of mental flow, or getting in the zone. Any accomplished person knows this to be true. So why is it that some managers insist on measuring others with a criteria based on how *the manager* likes to work, and not the worker? If they were not to see the worker sitting in his cubicle at such and such a time, or if they were not to see the person using the same particular approach as they, then the manager might become critical of the performance of the individual. They confuse *how* with *what*.

Managers who have not the advantage of refined leadership will think they can control the output of creative and professional work of a knowledge worker, and even their motivation, by controlling them physically. By controlling where they work, how they work, and when they work, the manager feels they are in control. But this is not so. Authority from above cannot dictate how one works best.

This brings us to another overarching principle, and one of my favorites:

Overarching Principle #18:

Activity of a knowledge worker, especially where creativity is involved, is best measured by results, not when, where, or how they work.

I once had an professor who posed this question: who of the following two people would you promote to a more senior level? Both accomplish the same amount of work, getting the same results for the company. One is constantly working long hours, if not at his desk, then in meetings, or running here and there with stacks of papers in hand, always in motion. The other works short hours, sits most of the day at his desk with his feet up, and is seen casually standing around conversing with others?   Now I exaggerated slightly, but of the two, who would you promote?

The answer is the one with his feet up on his desk. Remember what was stated: they both accomplish the same amount of work, getting the same results for the company. You might want to reward the other for hard work and punish the other for being lazy, but are you not committing the offense I opened this section describing, that is, judging individuals by only *how* they work and how they match what the manager sees as the right way to work?   By the way, the first worker, the one busy all the time has reached his or her upper level of ability by not having the right methods of being effective and efficient. He does not have enough SUBSTANCE, JOB, and STATURE left for more responsibility.

Effects of the big man

There are work environments where the manager has people working *for* him in the true sense. Either by plan when the manager has a controlling personality, or by default when the manager is the technical expert, and individuals become extensions of the manager who calls the shots. The subordinates are paralyzed in acting independently without direction or approval from their boss. This type of manager is referred to—not in a derogatory way, but in the effect produced—as the *big man*. One hears the following constantly from those working for this type of manager: "Let me ask Jim", "I am waiting for Jim to get back to me", "I can't just yet, Jim has my draft (or: report, drawing, calculation, proposed agenda, meeting minutes, test data) for his review and approval", "I will transfer you to him, only *Jim* knows the answer to that one", "I don't know, I am waiting to see Jim", and so on. Jim inadvertently has become a bottleneck and a suppressive force to growth for the individuals for whom he is responsible, and for the organization.

Individuals working under a big man become trained not to take on responsibility and are not held accountable. They find comfort in staying within the routine of JOB. The manager is accountable for everything outside the limited definition—imposed by the manager—of their responsibilities. Even if they would venture beyond, the individual would be guessing what would please the manager and what the manager would do, and not thinking expansively and independently on their own for their tasks at hand.

The solution to the big man syndrome is to practice refined leadership; its application being to have the opposite effect on individuals. If an individual were to feel a sense of importance or purpose, and would have the means to proceed, there would be a sense of freedom to act on their own. The model elements of Importance and Power are directly linked to Autonomy, and supported by the model component of MEANING; they all contribute to guarding against a manager inadvertently becoming the big man.

Scalable creative output

The ultimate benefit of Autonomy for the organization is the scalable effects for creative output of many individuals. You as a leader, despite your creative talents, are only one person with the limitations of time and energy of one person. Even if you were to transcend these limits, as a manager you would not be free from the administrative and non-technical burdens of your position. You could not step back to prepare your mind, or spend the time, for the creative process.

However, you can influence each of the individuals for whom you are responsible, helping them focus with a productively creative state of mind. Besides, the need for the creativity in the first place is for *their* tasks and for the many pronged incursions into CHALLENGE *they* make.

Managers of a business cannot directly predict and control ideas and actions that lead to breakthrough products or services, especially from top-down. Therefore, that which encourages many professionals to interact freely, to try things quickly, to explore new areas confidently, and to think independently, will promote a rich stream of new ideas, ultimately resulting in change and innovation. The flow of opportunity is from bottom-up, and from those who are cognizant of detail and the latest issues. In a market-driven, product-oriented, entrepreneurial organization, the model element of Autonomy allows and encourages interaction of individuals. This leads to energy and dynamism, the goal of a good leader, so that the quantity, quality, and fitness of ideas flows upward.

Where is the most fertile area in which ideas originate? The best source of new and useful ideas satisfies these two conditions: it is where the tinkering occurs at a working level; and it is where at that working level the need is understood the most. Tinkering is like thinking, being in the zone, but physically. It is the machine operator that keeps physically trying many ideas to solve one of his problems, until ultimately finding the next step in improvements for his work. It is the product user who modifies her product so it functions better to fit her requirements, or the sales engineer who offers customers solutions to slight variants of their needs and stumbles onto a big unmet need. The model element Autonomy allows this type of tinkering and exploration, which stems from the individual bringing a unique perspective in satisfying the two conditions above by using their unique background and skills.

But this type of freedom for an individual requires a positive environment and positive emotions for them to feel comfortable leaving the confines of the routine of JOB. This can be found in the model element of Importance.

ELEMENT: IMPORTANCE

Who would give more than 100% of themselves if what they were asked to work on were not important to the organization, or to themselves? And who would be driven to find a solution to the hardest problem, day and night, at work and in the car, interacting with others at all levels inside and outside of the organization, if they were to feel insignificant and not capable? And what if they would not feel they had it in them, or their self-image and self-confidence were negatively impacted? The answer is not me, not you, nobody—except the individual who just goes through the motions for appearances. The quickest way to create just a warm body of an individual for whom you are responsible is to restrict independence and to make them feel unimportant. The good news is that the reverse is true. The quickest way to create an energized individual is to make them feel important. Self-confidence becomes more crucial the further the individual ventures into the area of CHALLENGE.

Through refined leadership, you build the confidence and sense of importance in each one over whom you have influence. First, you need to sincerely appreciate everything they do; never minimize their input or accomplishments. Show how their work impacts the organization and Purpose. Importance is most influenced by your providing MEANING through Relationship. Recognizing the elements of SUBSTANCE of the individual is another factor in their feeling good about themselves and what they have to offer. To help make Relationship effective in this regard, you must deeply understand the individual, the circumstances surrounding the individual, and SUBSTANCE of that individual.

A micromanaging and know-it-all manager might react in certain ways to what an individual says that erodes self-image and confidence. At the very least, an individual who receives a negative response when they contribute to a discussion will be conditioned to be silent. The manager lecturing an individual with an annoyed attitude will have a similar effect. Responses to an individual, such as the following, said seriously or annoyed, should be avoided:

- "You don't understand, (then lecture)..."

- "Do I have to explain this again to you?"

- "You're wrong, (then lecture)..."

- "No!" (without any accompanying explanation)

- "Obviously you haven't been listening"

- "Obviously you haven't read my report"

- "Why can't you get this?"

Your aim as a refined leader is to allow them to be confident that they are good sources of information and that their ideas have value. They should feel comfortable, as if they can tell you anything. How could they be open with you, if they were to fear saying the wrong thing, much like from the big man syndrome described above in Autonomy? They need to be at ease with you, as a result of rapport and the model element Relationship. The following overarching principle applies here:

Overarching Principle #19:

To allow importance and autonomy of the individual and the bene-fits derived therefrom, always default to the assumption with each interaction that others are smarter and better informed than you.

Default to this assumption with each interaction, each day, with every person. If it turns out after you were to determine you know more, question and guide them, but never say "Why didn't you know that?" or "You should have known that." If appropriate, explain why and how not knowing adversely affects others or the organization, and how their behavior concerning the issue could improve their knowing for the future. Do all this in a friendly, relaxed way, and by no means appear to be lecturing a fellow professional.

An individual will be more willing to assume a responsibility and be accountable for that responsibility when they feel significance is attached to it and when emotionally their self-image and self-confidence is sufficient. Under these conditions, an individual takes on what is commonly described as *ownership*. The state of ownership is responsible for greater focus, more time devoted, higher commitment to decisions and trade-offs, and a greater sense of desire to succeed. With ownership, a higher level of initiative exists to arrive at an acceptable outcome for CHALLENGE and its elements: Unexplored, Chance, and Creativity.

ELEMENT: POWER

Other than the word *leadership*, the word *power* is next on the list of being overused and worn-out. History provides many examples of people using power. The famous ones we know about, however,

STATURE OF THE INDIVIDUAL   193

power does not have to be the product of, or the reason for, notoriety. Power does not have to be visible or obvious; its potency is more so when subtle and unseen. While the connotation for the word *leadership* is positive and constructive, the connotation for the word *power* is negative and destructive. With refined leadership, power is taken as positive, constructive, and sanctioned as a concept for the furtherance of good.

The use of Power in the context of refined leadership is as an element of STATURE, working in combination with the elements Autonomy and Importance; much like a position on the chess board where a simple combination of pieces determines advantage needed to win. Autonomy, Importance, and Power work together for increased STATURE of the individual. The individuals for whom you are responsible need the element Power to be active agents in getting things done, usually outside the routine of JOB. It involves going outside the standard structure or procedures, stepping over the line of their formal authority, and bending the rules, as needed. Simply working within established operations following standard procedures does not require the exercise of Power, but pushing into CHALLENGE of the refined leadership model does. To be effective in change and innovation, you will need to help the individual attain a sufficient amount of STATURE within the organization, along with its attendant model element of Power.

Sources of Influence

As you would expect, formal authority within an organization provides weight to have your requests carried out. This formal authority can derive from title, such as CEO or Vice President of Marketing, or functional position, such as Sr. Project Manager or as a subject matter expert with a descriptive formal title.   However, from a bottom-up perspective, and in the realm of refined leadership in less hierarchical settings, Power is exerted in organizations from individuals with no formal authority. Authority other than formal is the type that is assumed by individuals. It is relative and dynamic, and dependent on the situation.

Power exercised through a forcing control has a negative feel and causes push back from others. Controlling and micromanaging to exert Power leads to the individual trying to be the smartest person in the room, and as was discussed previously, this is not possible. Consequently, this approach thwarts Autonomy and Importance of others. Overt forcefulness from anyone weakens the outward, positive effects of Power, while the opposite is true: a subtle Power from strength of character and other good qualities of the individual exerting that Power, makes for an inherent control through Purpose, Standards, and fellowship.

How can you instill or induce the model element of Power in the individual for whom you are responsible? What unique quality can be found within SUBSTANCE of the individual from which they can benefit? How can each component and element of the model of leadership contribute to Power? The following highlights some of the factors in relationship to the model and refined leadership that may help the individual for whom you are responsible exercise an ability to get things done:

- From MEANING
  - ▸ high purpose
  - ▸ relationships with others
  - ▸ connections
  - ▸ business perspective
  - ▸ team/fellowship

- From SUBSTANCE
  - conscientiousness/follow-up/follow-through
  - desire/drive
  - judgment from experience
  - persuasiveness
  - communication
  - decisiveness
  - vision, seeing clearly
  - charisma/persona
  - refined leadership skills

- From JOB
  - formal position/title
  - veto or approval
  - expert knowledge
  - transactional knowledge
  - historical perspective
  - access to customer/parts of value chain

- From CHALLENGE
  - ad hoc formal position/title
  - assumed position/title
  - awareness of events
  - teaming skills
  - energy level/activity involvement
  - reporting/visibility
  - assumption of responsibility
  - use of creativity
  - comfortable with risk

- From STATURE
  - freedom to act
  - importance of tasks
  - self-confidence
  - reputation
  - knowing/playing the game
  - good at politics

The above lists are all the facets of Power, the source from which an individual can draw to get things done. For a given individual at a given time and place, for a particular situation, any combination of the sources above could be effective. Understanding (Chapter 2) is needed throughout the exercise of Power, its tactics, and its game-like nature. Knowing how far one can go beyond the norms of the organization requires a practicality guided by a moral compass. The individual may need your help at times in moving the ball forward without going too far out of bounds.

Power can be from formal organizational authority, but even then, the user of Power still needs to assume it on their own. For whether it is given or taken, it is in the reaction by others that confirms that authority, thus making Power effective. This is the transactional nature of the model element Power.

Power Appropriate to Purpose

How far can an individual go to get what they want? What they want should be in line with the goals of CHALLENGE and Purpose. Power is only appropriate when within the bounds of Purpose, the reason for the work. It begs the question *do the ends justify the means*? The answer is yes, if it were within the Purpose of MEANING, stated or implied, and Purpose fell within the ethics espoused by the organization. These ethics dictate the limits of Power, or to what lengths one can go to get things done. Your moral obligation then becomes to work for an organization in which you can believe.

In the refined leadership model, Power is balanced and constrained by Purpose. However, just like fictitious restrictions in Creativity, you will run into fictitious barriers to Power. The deeper you go into CHALLENGE, the further you will push the limits to succeed by overcoming fictitious barriers to authority. The true boundaries are revealed by MEANING, that is, the ethical understanding as imposed by Purpose.

The following is an example of the use of Power. Consider a crisis situation where a machine in manufacturing is down, stopping all production. It is not inappropriate or unethical for you to drop everything and go to the local hardware store to buy a part for the machine, if Purpose included maintaining production to meet deliveries to customers. However, in this situation there are limits. It would be inappropriate to steal money from petty cash, or to steal the part from the local hardware store. Maybe it might be all right to bypass the purchasing procedures to buy the part. But what if there were another constraint on Power through a different Purpose, say, keeping control of all machine repairs for safety reasons in a nuclear power plant, then bypassing the purchasing procedures to buy the part would not be appropriate.

Consider one thing further; what if a life were at risk in the situation of the above example, say, someone caught in the machine? Now breaking any kind of rule or even commandeering a part in an unauthorized manner could be condoned, even as far as making you a hero for saving a life. Exerting Power, going around the system, needs to be appropriate with the situation in the context of Purpose.

A Sense of the Game

Power does not mean forcing or commanding, or winning at another's expense, but it does mean influencing circumstances through situation or transaction to allow you to move forward toward your goal. You and the individuals for whom you are responsible should always strive for a win/win outcome, and therefore, never think in terms of adversarial positions. You may have others that unwittingly do not help the win/win outcome, but they are not your enemies.

The adversary with which you are dealing is that of the universe, its natural laws, and unexpected random events. The elements of game theory are reserved for your decision making and for dealing with possible alternate outcomes against this natural adversary. Against her, Fortuna, you are always playing to win.

As they say, you will need to know the name of the game. Power could be too blunt of a tool when you do not use your understanding (see Chapter 2) at how to play that game. It does not matter the degree of Power you have through the various sources available to you, you will still need strategy for the bigger picture and longer term, and you will need tactics for the encounters at hand. This is how you, and the individuals for whom you are responsible, will find and keep your direction through the area of CHALLENGE. The following overarching principle summarizes the lack of certainty in outcomes, but the important role of focus, depth of thought, and persistence for acceptable results:

Overarching Principle #20:

One cannot guarantee not to lose by doing everything right in a win-win manner. Not failing requires a sense that one is in a game, and one is in it to win.

There is a scene in the movie *Havana*[2] with Robert Redford that is a good illustration of Power, tactics, and a winning philosophy. The main character is a gambler in Cuba as the government is in a struggle against the rebels led by Fidel Castro. In one scene sitting at the table in a bar, Redford's love interest in the movie is speaking with him along with her husband who is trying to get Redford to help in the rebel's cause. Robert Redford's character resists;

he is not interested in politics, but is accused of not understanding. The dialogue picks up from there:

Redford: "Hey. I know politicians, OK?
            I play cards with them.
            And I love to, 'cause they're easy to beat.
            It's the only place an ordinary man can beat a
            politician."

            [He makes a motion to leave. The women is
            visibly agitated and makes an effort to keep
            him from leaving with a hurried question.]

Women: "Why are they easy to beat?"

Redford: "Because sometimes in poker
            it's smarter to lose with a winning hand
            so you can win later with a losing one. See?
            And politicians never quite believe that
            'cause they want power now."

Why is this pertinent? Robert Redford's character understood the game, and he had tactics within an overall philosophy of giving up immediate gain for the bigger picture. However, his opponents did not understand the nature of winning this particular game. They were familiar with naked power, and taking what they could, when they could, according to Redford's character. Patience, timing, and a sense of the rhythm of this game was beyond their understanding. Behavior, demeanor, actions, words, and emotional reactions are part of the tactics in the game of poker, similar to many transactional situations in the business world.

How to win is not apparent at first. You can specifically state what constitutes success for an endeavor; it can be defined. What you cannot be precise about is knowing how you will actually get there. The further out in time and the more complex the project, the less one knows of what will transpire along the way. This is directly related to topic of Chance (see Chapter 5) and to know-how embedded in the organization (see Chapter 7). All you can hope for is to have a general idea of the direction you will take. I believe it was Dwight Eisenhower when commanding the Allied forces in WWII who said that the value in a plan was not the plan itself, but the process of planning. Endeavors rarely go as planned, however, one is more prepared for contingency actions from the process of planning and from thinking the plan through. The process of planning forces deeper understanding of the difficulties that lie ahead. The main danger is being very wrong in overall direction of the plan. To succeed even by being flexible during execution of the plan, you still have to be approximately correct.

Condition where no winning is possible

No winning is possible where Power is exerted by authority that is unaware of necessary trade-offs, or even the need itself for trade-offs. One cannot do all and have all perfect, and if that were the definition of succeeding, then no success would ever be possible, not in a world of economic scarcity and limits on time. Trading-off is balancing, and balancing is the essence of viability, or the ability to survive and live by functioning properly where needed the most. A manager, an individual, a group, or a team must have and maintain a working-level perspective with respect to what they can and cannot do. The trade-offs and balancing are necessary, and as a refined leader you must understand their importance.

Consider the example of an executive moving from a high level position in a multi-billion dollar company to a high level position in a small company. My bet is that the executive will have trouble being successful, not for the reason the larger environment is more bureaucratic and the smaller is more entrepreneurial, but for the reason of his lack of understanding of the balance within his new business and the trade-offs required to succeed. He will not have understanding of the role certain trade-offs play, since he rarely had to make them at his previous position; there he may have had ample resources and time in relation to his definition of winning. He never felt obliged to constantly balance his resources and time, or to have more than a little regard for cost. Somehow (and luckily) a few individuals at a working level out of the hundreds reporting to him did this without his awareness. He would now have to make these trade-offs himself. That leads to the next overarching principle:

Overarching Principle #21:

There are never enough resources or time to accomplish anything until there is accountability for making decisions based on trade-offs. Any definition of success is grounded on this balancing.

A good example in everyday life of Overarching Principle #21 is in personal decisions. Consider a child growing up in affluence and he is given everything he wants. The parents do not think it important for the child to make choices, such as choosing this or that, but not both, thus developing a sense of scarcity. Nothing is off limits requiring trade-offs, and no understanding is being developed around the concept of delayed gratification, or the concept of not consuming now in exchange for much more in the future. The child never has to use that type of thinking. Though he may find himself in a personal financial situation as an adult where he could not afford it, he will probably have trouble not buying the biggest and best of everything. This person will have trouble making trade-offs and modifying his definition of success.

Another example is the CEO who pushes the company for more new products in crash time projects, but does not make allowances in expectations for the higher risks of design or manufacturing defects, or market introduction problems. He does not make the trade-offs between expectations (same level of quality), time and resources. The individuals leading the crash time projects on a working level are the ones who face the reality of making these trade-offs.

THE POLITICAL CONUNDRUM

Consider the following statements: "live and let live" and "kill or be killed". One is the law of civilization, the other the law of the jungle. How can the following two ideas be reconciled by the refined leader, and should they? How about when one does not want to loose when being politically attacked with their career at risk, and yet, does not want to stoop to a thug's level in response? How can the leader keep from giving up a philosophy of management that more accurately states "grow and let grow?" It is a fine line to walk. First, you must recognize when you have an adversary thrust upon you. It might not be obvious, although you will come to suspect by telltale words and actions. Use the process for deep understanding from Chapter 2 to confirm you have an adversary.

Second, you match STATURE, yours and those for whom you are responsible, to your adversary's. If your STATURE were greater in the organization than your adversary, then practicing pure refined leadership would be the solution to the conundrum. If your adversary's STATURE were equal or greater than yours, then you need to find ways to increase your STATURE and that of your fellowship (see Overarching Principle #7).

In a political environment, you can widen the circle of those having a stake in the issue at your peer level and above by publicly revealing the facts, and explaining clearly how it affects them. You could take advantage of the fellowship built around you by using your leadership to increase their STATURE and their influence for good. But these approaches do not guarantee that you can control the destructive effects of those bent on your defeat.

If the political infighting were widespread, and if upper management were to allow destructive personal attacks, then the organization would be culturally in trouble. Your influence as a leader becomes more important than ever for those of whom you are responsible by providing STATURE to them. Unfortunately, your vulnerability in practicing refined leadership will be ammunition for your adversaries—that is the conundrum.

If you do not have a immediate superior in your organization who understands and supports you in what you are doing as a leader, then you should restrict your practice of refined leadership to the people and groups for whom you have authority and can trust. I relied heavily on Operating Principle #7, and it worked to some degree, when I found myself in a thug-like atmosphere with going-behind-the-back detractors. However, it was not enough. I lost the political battle.

Defeating your adversaries in the political arena may be necessary at times. The following quote from Sun Tzu, *The Art of War*, translated by Samuel B. Griffith, is appropriate:

> Anciently the skilful [sic] warriors first made themselves invincible and awaited the enemy's moment of vulnerability...   Invincibility depends on one's self;

the enemy's vulnerability on him... It follows that those skilled in war can make themselves invincible but cannot cause an enemy to be certainly vulnerable... Therefore it is said that one may know how to win, but cannot necessarily do so... Invincibility lies in the defence; the possibility of victory in the attack.[3]

If your winning is good for the organization, then you may have to exploit a win/lose outcome with respect to the adversary, even though you are pursuing a win/win outcome for the company. At best you can neutralize your adversary. From Sun Tzu,

For to win one hundred victories in one hundred battles is not the acme of skill... To subdue the enemy without fighting is the acme of skill... Thus, what is of supreme importance in war is to attack the enemy's strategy.[4]

You will run into this political conundrum, I assure you. Practice refined leadership, but confront the thug by matching your enemy's desire to harm you with an equal, or greater, resistance for your own defense. Bring out truth for all to see; however, this does not work without the support of those in higher authority. The ultimate danger to you in this environment is that you drift to a management style opposite that of a refined leadership, out of necessity.

CHAPTER 9

CRITICAL INTERFACES

"Nevertheless he ought to be slow to believe and to act, nor should he himself show fear, but proceed in a temperate manner with prudence and humanity, so that too much confidence may not make him incautious and too much distrust render him intolerable.

"Upon this a question arises: whether it be better to be loved than feared or feared than loved?"

Niccolo Machiavelli, The Prince[1]

The implementation of the refined leadership model comes down to interaction with individuals, plain and simple. Most of this interaction occurs at interfaces between elements of the model, much of which has been covered in the previous chapters. In this chapter, guidelines for applying the refined leadership model using the four critical interfaces are reviewed and summarized in one place. This will help you use the model for a given individual as a set of interactions. You may want to correlate each interface with traditional, and more recognizable, managerial procedures and practices. For example, the annual review process is associated with the Relationship-Standards Interface, a personal improvement plan with the Capabilities-Responsibilities Interface, and formal project plans, such as in the form of a Gantt or PERT chart, with the Practice-Autonomy Interface. Understanding these interfaces in terms of their traditional form will help you in your goal of seamlessly working the ideas of refined leadership into your organization and for the model to become second nature to you.

RELATIONSHIP-STANDARDS INTERFACE

As covered in Chapter 4, building a relationship with an individual is not only for the purpose of understanding that individual, but for the individual to understand what your expectations are of him or her. It is also needed to have Standards provide balance and constraints for Relationship. The Relationship-Standard Interface is critical in this regard. This interface is shown in the refined leadership model in Figure 3.2 (p.45) as the elements Relationship and Standards connected by a common underline.

For a leader to be effective, he or she should exhibit firmness at the right moments, yet be flexible when required, and for this to occur, the two elements of Relationship and Standards must co-exist as countervailing forces. Although flexibility will come about from the action of other elements of the model, such as Autonomy and Power, the immediate interplay between firmness and flexibility is in the Relationship-Standards Interface.

Through the Relationship-Standards Interface, overall standards are set by the leader for the individual that are consistent for all the individuals for whom the leader is responsible. Also, specific to the individual through this interface is the two-way communication aligning the individual's innate standards with your expectations associated with satisfying Responsibilities of JOB. It is here where trust and loyalty is established from mutual responsibility, accountability, and truthfulness.

The following are guidelines that use the ideas and principles of refined leadership in the area of the Relationship-Standards Interface:

- Both understand, identify, and agree on expectations

- Have dialogue often for leader's support in specific situations

- Determine individual's internal standards; allow them to govern when higher than externally imposed standards

- Establish rapport during frequent one-on-one meetings

- Keep relationship appropriate with Standards delimiting the relationship;

- Control based on results and feedback, not by how the work is done, or micromanaging, or dictating tasks

- Reprimand based on standards according to situation, behavior, and impact; always kept positive and private; in these ways it does not become personal

- Us as conduit for providing MEANING (Purpose and Relationship, see Chapter 4) and knowing and influencing SUBSTANCE (Standards, Person, and Capabilities, see Chapter 6)

You should note that this interface is a valuable tool in balancing your relationship with the individual. By using the opposing force of standards and expectations (those you impose and those you recognize as internal to the individual), you keep the relationship appropriately professional and to a proper level or depth.

With the Relationship-Standards Interface, you keep control and authority without the need for obvious, intrusive, and non-professional reprimanding. In this manner, you can be demanding with stretch goals without being petty by micromanaging or being domineering. In addition, with this interface you learn what is important to the individual, what matters to him or her, so you can connect that with what matters to you and the organization. By providing MEANING through this interface, you tie what they care about to motivation.

What of the question posed by Niccolo Machiavelli in the chapter quotation above? Is it better for a leader to be loved or feared? The following is his answer in his own words:

> It may be answered that one should wish to be both, but, because it is difficult to unite them in one person, it is much safer to be feared than loved, when, of the two, either [must] be dispensed with.[2]

Later he summarizes his arguments,

> ... men loving according to their own will and fearing according to that of the prince, a wise prince should establish himself on that which is in his own control and not in that of others; he must endeavour only to avoid hatred...[3]

The answer he provides is that it is better to be feared than loved because love can be fleeting with circumstances, but in no way is it good to be despised. Love can easily evaporate when self-interest is tested. This seems to contradict refined leadership principles. The answer I prescribe to the question is that it is better neither to be loved nor feared. Love is not necessary and fear negatively affects everything refined leadership teaches us. Fear displaces the higher functioning of the brain used for analysis and creativity. Individuals cannot function in a state of fear, or be open or truthful, or have the relationships required for achievement in the realm of CHALLENGE. I say replace "it is much safer to be feared than loved" with "it is much safer to be respected as the accepted leader toward a common purpose." That type of leadership is in everyone's self-interest to follow. Always respected, and maybe sometimes admired, you should hope to be a good example to those for whom you are responsible. But that is it; expect no more, and hope for no less.

CAPABILITIES-RESPONSIBILITIES INTERFACE

With this interface, you will determine what additional knowledge and skills are needed by the individual. By understanding what constitutes competency for the model component of JOB, you will address the need for adding to the individual's Capabilities. The degree to which the individual accepts the need for self-improvement in these areas is highly dependent on his or her personality and innate drive (model element Standards). You will need to be an expert yourself in the specialty and profession of the individual, or you will need to rely on your ability to come to understand by using the ideas and principles presented in Chapter 2, *Understanding, Before All*

Else. Spending time with the individual and expending effort is necessary to fully understand their abilities in connection with JOB. This can be done in concert with the Relationship-Standards Interface. You should actively look for the tasks the individual can do well, so you can build from those strengths. This interface is shown in the refined leadership model in Figure 3.2 (p.45) as the elements Capabilities and Responsibilities connected by a common underline.

The following are guidelines that use the ideas and principles of refined leadership in the area of the Capabilities-Responsibilities Interface:

- Both identify and agree on responsibilities associated with individual's work

- Explore individual's total abilities; find deficiencies with respect to responsibilities and required competencies

- Obtain agreement on the need for improvement; does it match individual's internal standards

- Help the individual visualize what they ultimately want to become

- Provide on-going education and training; find lessons learned from each experience of the individual

- Use as conduit for knowing and influencing SUBSTANCE (Standards, Person, and Capabilities, see Chapter 6) and configuring JOB (Responsibilities, Practice, and Capacity, see Chapter 7)

Holding the individual accountable for that which they are responsible will promote growth in all the elements of SUBSTANCE. It is important you support the individual, especially when they take the route through CHALLENGE to add to Capabilities.

You as leader must use all the elements of the model of leadership to encourage and reassure the individual, therefore helping to build and maintain confidence. You will affect learning, as well as work-related performance, by providing MEANING by your interaction, much the same as a teacher in school does for her students. Have you ever spent effort on a homework assignment because the teacher was going to collect it? You worked hard to make her feel proud of what you learned. And if she did not collect it, you were disappointed. She provided MEANING for your learning.

PRACTICE-AUTONOMY INTERFACE

As covered in previous chapters, advancing entrepreneurial change or pushing the envelope of innovation occurs with individuals and teams moving into the realm of CHALLENGE, and not by conforming to standards, procedures, and rules. The larger the proportion of the organization's workforce that is confined to the routine of JOB required for executing business compared to that on project teams in the realm of Challenge, then the more a bureaucratic-type inertia is a factor in bringing about change and innovation. The leadership model elements of Autonomy and Power are the antidote of red tape. With the Practice-Autonomy Interface, you allow the individual the freedom to work how they wish and in the way they need in order to reach their optimum when dealing with Unexplored, Chance, and Creativity. This interface is shown in the refined leadership model in Figure 3.2 (p.45) as the elements Practice and Autonomy connected by a common underline.

How do you allow the maximum degree of Autonomy while maintaining the necessary conformance to rules and procedures? You do this by allowing almost anything while the individual and the team is in the model region of CHALLENGE, and you ask for conformance when their activities affect the existing business and JOB.

The following are guidelines that use the ideas and principles of refined leadership in the area of the Practice-Autonomy Interface:

- Give autonomy, but follow progress without being obvious; watch for actions going off course into potential trouble

- Allow freedom from routine required for creative results; increase variation (opposite of what required for achieving quality); look to move market, product, process, technology, and organization

- Require team performance against a rough short-term plan instead of precise long-term plan

- Have contingency points associated with testing or uncertainty; have contingency actions planned

- Draw out all from the elements Person and Capabilities of SUBSTANCE of individual; look to uniqueness

- Couple Autonomy of individual and team with Importance and Power for synergistic effect

- Use as conduit for knowing and influencing STATURE (Autonomy, Importance, and Power, see Chapter 8), configuring JOB (Responsibilities, Practice, and Capacity, see Chapter 7), and addressing CHALLENGE (Unexplored, Chance, Creativity, see Chapter 5).

As leader, your creativity will be needed to find ways to balance the freedom you give the individual and minimizing the effects on the ongoing business. If the individual were separated from daily activities associated with JOB, then Autonomy becomes less of an issue. This is the idea behind a self-directed, cross-functional team. The team members dedicate 100% of their time working on the project and for the team.

The following is a quote from Henry Ford from his autobiography, *My Life and Work*. You can associate this with the frame of mind of individuals on a team when they have freedom from the standard operations of the business:

> This may seem haphazard, but it is not. A group of men, wholly intent upon getting work done, have no difficulty in seeing that the work is done. They do not get into trouble about the limits of authority, because they are not thinking of titles.[4]

The critical interface of Practice with Autonomy is the principal path connecting JOB with STATURE. It balances and limits freedom from becoming impractical, or greatly inappropriate, with respect to what is standard and customary. STATURE determines the likelihood of success in the realm of CHALLENGE for the individual. On the other side of STATURE, you balance and limit Power with Purpose, one of the elements of MEANING.

POWER-PURPOSE INTERFACE

Opposite the Practice-Autonomy Interface between JOB and STATURE is the Power-Purpose Interface between STATURE and MEANING.

As discussed in Chapter 8, in the realm of CHALLENGE—where no clear solutions are available and from where creation and change result—the ability to get things done through the use of Power is essential. However, like Autonomy, Power must be balanced and have limits. This is provided by the countervailing force of Purpose. This interface is shown in the refined leadership model in Figure 3.2 (p.45) as the elements Power and Purpose connected by a common underline

When you, and the individuals for whom you are responsible, approach difficult tasks by going outside the norm using bold strategy and aggressive tactics, you must stay within limits of appropriateness and propriety. Your actions must be consistent with Purpose; in this way, Power is balanced and checked by Purpose. The following are guidelines that use the ideas and principles of refined leadership in the area of the Power-Purpose Interface:

- Monitor actions to assure they are appropriate

- Use Purpose through Relationship to connect to the use of Power by individual and team

- Have and communicate vision, see clearly, and have a strong element of strategy; vision connects Power and Purpose.

- Encourage a healthy amount of risk taking; protect individual from consequences of failures

- Assure Purpose as communicated conforms with the organization's code of ethics

- Use as conduit for knowing and influencing STATURE (Autonomy, Importance, and Power, see Chapter 8), and addressing CHALLENGE (Unexplored, Chance, Creativity, see Chapter 5).

As with Autonomy, you as leader allow the level of Power that the individual exercises. Decisions made and actions taken will increase the STATURE of the individual as perceived by others, especially when not associated with JOB. You as leader have a direct influence on increasing the individual's STATURE by allowing increasing levels of Power, using your judgment in determining the levels of decision making and action permissible. If the individual were to possess a good degree of competency, and you both were to share closely an understanding of Purpose, then his or her level of assumed authority could rise to your level. He or she would then approach being your proxy in Power, and possibly be factored into the succession plan as a candidate for your replacement.

CHAPTER *10*

CONCLUSION

"...the Lord did not create people as 'resources' for organization. They do not come in proper size and shape for the tasks that have to be done in organization—and they cannot be machined down or recast for these tasks. People are always 'almost fits' at best."

Peter Drucker, The Effective Executive[1]

M uch of the thinking in business and industry concerning leadership of organizations revolves around strategy. In the academic area of technology management and in the world of corporate consulting, it is the larger pieces of the strategic puzzle for obtaining competitive advantage that get the attention. Scrutiny of upper management tends to stay at this strategic level of the business and away from the working level where capabilities, know-how, and technology reside. And when discussion at the strategic level involves technical matters in connection with markets, competition, and finances, it can only be in general terms at the 35,000 foot level.

Upper management stays informed with the help of those who have a deep understanding of the know-how available to the organization.   A bottom-up perspective permits executive decisions and corporate strategy to be workable.   Connecting with the business side of the organization should be one of your responsibilities in your role as engineering leader, or technical manager.   The elements in the model, especially those within MEANING, CHALLENGE, and JOB, should help point you in the right direction.   Chapter 2, *Understanding, Before All Else*, should also help as it does in general when working with the model of leadership.

The smallest detail is handled by the base unit of the organization, the individual.   Similar to fractals where the shape on a small scale is indistinguishable to that on a large scale (an example is the shape and form of cloud cover over a whole continent being of the same characteristic shape as the smallest cloud), an organization will have a look and feel, and will operate with a competency, that is much the same as the individuals doing the work.   This concept of individual as base unit can also apply to change and innovation.   The next breakthrough product or service may have its beginnings as an idea, or an unexpected discovery, by a lone individual or by a few interacting individuals.   In this regard, the future of the organization could hinge on the unlikely survival of one fragile, nascent idea at the working level.   Aspects of corporate strategy could ultimately be indistinguishable from the detail of that one idea from that one individual employee.   But here is where the value of refined leadership and the model of leadership are needed most: both the idea and the individual are a product of Chance and Creativity.   There are no guarantees that change or innovation will occur.   What the organization is and what it becomes is dependent on small detail and inspired individuals.

THE POTENTIALITY OF THE INDIVIDUAL

When it comes to the individual, the idea that perception is reality could not be more accurate. People are judged by others with every encounter by what is seen on the outside. It takes time and energy to know someone, and coming to know someone is built into the refined leadership model with Relationship and the other model elements of SUBSTANCE. However, it is not SUBSTANCE that is affected by perception, but STATURE. It is by a mismatch of STATURE with SUBSTANCE that an individual's future performance would surprise you either on the upside in a pleasing way, or on the downside in a disappointing way. With the routine of JOB, you know you will keep seeing much of the same performance, but with the uncertainty of CHALLENGE, the individual is tested to the point of revealing more.

It is not a valid idea that you can define an individual by statistics, that is, where they are in a normal distribution, or where they fall on the bell curve. Maybe with height or weight, but not with the innumerable and unknowable variables that affect outcomes in CHALLENGE from the invisible contributions of SUBSTANCE, the transient nature of STATURE, and the inspiration from MEANING. To have a measurement for every area or intricacy of knowledge, skill, and judgment is not only impractical, it is impossible. First, the criteria for measurement must be right, and then the assessment against that criteria must be right. I have seen in practice how this leaves room for large error from a narrow mental model (tunnel vision) for criteria and from bias (perception is reality) for the assessment.

This is what makes leading so much more difficult than managing. Classifying and measuring is a good concept for managing, but a bad concept for leading. In managing you measure to get better, but in leading you are in areas where no history is available from which to measure. Managing sees everything as precise and analyzable. The less emotional content the better. Leading sees possibilities with the individuals, and the more emotion the better. Managing weeds out individuals based on the routine of JOB, even the individual with exceptional skills unrelated to Responsibilities. Leading finds and grows individuals in the realm of CHALLENGE. Managing can be closed ended, while leading is always open ended.

The consideration of the individual as the base unit of know-how is connected to the engineer as a professional, and essential for a state of professionalism. Professionals are personally accountable for their knowledge, skills, and judgment, and for the discharge of their responsibilities. The resultant individualism of the professional can be relied upon to instill a sense of liability. This creates a conscientiousness in upholding their end of work at a high level of quality. Refined leadership is founded on the belief in the individual as a professional, but even the non-professional conforms to the components and elements of the model of leadership.

TURN THE MODEL ON YOURSELF

All the actionable elements are in the refined leadership model for you to use in interacting with each individual for whom you are responsible, but there is another on which to turn the model. Are you not eminently responsible for yourself? Make an effort at understanding yourself by looking inwardly and objectively. Develop a snapshot of the leadership model for yourself. You cannot lead others if you cannot lead yourself; there is no individual you should know better.

The model of leadership is a great guide for self-development. It can help you become more rounded, focused, aware, and assured by following its direction. Use it as a tool to gain confidence when managing—and leading—upward. Promotion within your organization will depend on your growth as a manager and leader.

PEOPLE, AFTER ALL ELSE

The model of refined leadership is an antidote for gender, age, race, or nationality bias. The model is blind to any personal characteristic other than SUBSTANCE of the individual, JOB qualifications and performance, and STATURE within the organization. Refined leadership is based on seeing the strengths and the value in individual uniqueness. But above all, the model element of Relationship affords the opportunity to discovery what we have in common as people.

Civility is the rule when interacting with people. Always keep an encounter positive. Start from where the individual is with respect to their ideas or opinions. Only after fully understanding the other's position, and if possible their interests—behind every position are interests—then state your position. Never argue, be polite, always making the other feel important. Stay true to your interests (if you both should share the same higher purpose or immediate goal, then your interests should be similar). If it does not matter to you, just agree. If you both cannot agree, and the situation dictates you must, then agree to try to find a solution through being creative together. The foregoing suggestions are not easy to follow, but following them are part of refined leadership.

When you show civility to others, you should expect civility in return, and if not from just anybody, then from your peers, your boss, and those higher in the organization. Do not allow yourself to be subjected to degrading behavior, especially from your boss. The last overarching principle follows:

Overarching Principle #22:

Never sacrifice your dignity, self-esteem, or belief
in yourself for any reason, but most of all,
do not ask those you lead to sacrifice theirs.

There were times in my career when I questioned whether a job was worth the degrading atmosphere and treatment. Even though I had a young family and was dependent on the income, I set for myself a trigger point when I would take action to correct the situation, when things would have gone too far. There are always alternatives in a country that values personal liberty, private property, the rule of law, and free enterprise.

By remembering that the failure of an individual, or a team, in the pursuit of an endeavor is the failure of not those individuals, but of the leadership, then you will make it your responsibility to not find fault or place blame. If you were to tell me the story of a failed project and you allowed me a few questions, I could trace the cause back to poor leadership. If the perception of yourself were that of a leader, as it should be, then anytime you do not take total responsibility you are not only at risk of failing yourself, but of failing those who look to you for that leadership.

Remember that an individual for whom you are responsible, and people in general, will respond emotionally to your interaction with them either positively or negatively. Only you can control the interactions to make that response an emotionally positive one, and in turn to have a positive affect on their performance. Owing to the fact that a technical organization is a people concoction, each individual you influence interacts with and influences other individuals, thus affecting the performance of everyone. As a leader, you have the ultimate impact on the chemistry between individuals, the spirit of the team, or the atmosphere of the work space.

An engineer, or any knowledge worker, works in their head, where the effort cannot be observed. You as leader have a big effect on whether they are thinking the right way about the right things. By your influence, you open their thinking to the higher functioning parts of their brain for creativity and analysis. Your encouragement allows them to convert those abstract thoughts into concrete plans for effective action. You cannot do their work for them; you can only provide the fertile environment for that work. Once this becomes second nature to you, you will be a model of leadership.

LIST OF OVERARCHING PRINCIPLES

#1: Make every effort to understand, then decide and act; but first, fully understand. (p. 20)

#2: No decision is effective or useful until sound judgment is applied to an appropriate objective within a higher purpose, and accepted by those who are responsible for implementation. (p. 36)

#3: A connection made, and maintained, between the technical and the business sides of the organization attaches value to the work of a technical professional. (p. 60)

#4: Leadership is a unique relationship between two people, repeated as many times as necessary. The leader is responsible to make this relationship positive and meaningful, no matter the difficulties. (p. 65)

#5: A positive emotional state promotes creativity, expressiveness, commitment, and an absorption into work. (p. 68)

#6: No trust or loyalty can exist without a two-way commitment to, and communication of, responsibility, accountability, and truthfulness. (p. 81)

#7: A fellowship will arise around good leadership, especially to pursue a higher purpose and a call to challenge. In this environment, no one cares who gets the credit, making anything possible. (p. 91)

#8: An acceptance that every activity has a rhythm and a timing, and a sense of such, is the basis for patience and perseverance. (p. 97)

#9: In order to improve conclusions and decisions, expand the associated tacit model for the endeavor by relaxing focus and specialization. No accepted truth is safe from new data. (p. 112)

#10:   Distinguish between negative and positive random events, searching actively for the positive random events, learning from them and using them to your advantage. (p. 115)

#11:   Because of randomness, limited resources, and time, nothing in life or work is perfect, and if it were, nothing would stay perfect; therefore, define perfection realistically. (p. 119)

#12:   Innovation is encouraged by and is made possible through supportive, collaborative exploration, and with a desire to learn from failure. (p. 126)

#13: Self-improvement is not possible until there is an acceptance of the need by the individual and the adoption of a new internalized standard. (p. 146)

#14: No person, group, or team will ever appear good enough until there is a bias in perception toward strengths. (p. 154)

#15: No probability of success is high until there is an appropriate set of individuals, with the right capabilities, accepting the challenge as a true team. (p. 168)

#16: Know-how and technology are tacit and informal, residing in the heads of individuals. Yet when formalized, both still need to be in the heads of those effectively using them; it becomes their craft. (p. 172)

#17: As a leader, one grows stronger by allowing vulnerability; one will only <u>seem</u> weak by making others appear strong. (p. 184)

#18: Activity of a knowledge worker, especially where creativity is involved, is best measured by results, not when, where, or how they work. (p. 186)

#19: To allow importance and autonomy of the individual and the benefits derived therefrom, always default to the assumption with each interaction that others are smarter and better informed than you. (p. 192)

#20: One cannot guarantee not to lose by doing everything right in a win-win manner. Not failing requires a sense that one is in a game, and one is in it to win. (p. 198)

#21: There are never enough resources or time to accomplish anything until there is accountability for making decisions based on trade-offs. Any definition of success is grounded on this balancing. (p. 201)

#22: Never sacrifice your dignity, self-esteem, or belief in yourself for any reason, but most of all, do not ask those you lead to sacrifice theirs. (p. 222)

NOTES

Chapter 1

[1] Dumas, Alexandre, *The Count of Monte Cristo* (Oxford: Oxford University Press, 1990)

Chapter 2

[1] Hume, David, *An Enquiry Concerning Human Understanding, 2nd ed.* (Indianapolis: Hackett Publishing Co., 1993)

Chapter 3

[1] Labaree, Leonard W., Ketcham, Ralph L., Boatfield, Helen C, & Fineman, Helene H. (Eds.), *The Autobiography of Benjamin Franklin, 2nd ed.* (New Haven: Yale University Press, 1964)

Chapter 4

[1] Smith, Adam, *The Wealth of Nations* (New York: Alfred A. Knopf, 1991)

[2] Labaree, Leonard W., Ketcham, Ralph L., Boatfield, Helen C, & Fineman, Helene H. (Eds.), *The Autobiography of Benjamin Franklin, 2nd ed.* (New Haven: Yale University Press, 1964)

Chapter 5

[1] Griffith, Samuel B. (Trans.), *Sun Tzu: The Art of War* (Oxford: Oxford University Press, 1993)

[2] Ibid.

[3] Marriott, W. K. (Trans.), Niccolo Machiavelli, *The Prince* (New York: Alfred A. Knopf, 1992)

[4] Darwin, Charles, *The Origin of Species* (New York: Random House, 1993)

Chapter 6

[1] Caldwell, Bruce (Ed.), Collected Works of F. A. Hayek, *The Road to Serfdom: Text and Documents, The Definitive Edition* (London: The University of Chicago Press, 2007)

[2] *The Bridge on the River Kwai,* Produced by Sam Spiegel, Directed by David Lean (Culver City, CA: Columbia Pictures, 1957, renewed 1985)

[3] Drucker, Peter F., *The Effective Executive* (New York: Harper & Row, 1985)

Chapter 7

[1] Ford, Henry, *My Life and Work: An Autobiography of Henry Ford* (BN Publishing, 2008)

Chapter 8

[1] Melville, Herman, *Moby Dick* (New York: Penguin Books, 2003)

[2] *Havana,* Produced by Sydney Pollack and Richard Roth, Directed by Sydney Pollack (Universal City, CA: Universal Pictures, 1990)

Chapter 9

[1] Marriott, W. K. (Trans.), Niccolo Machiavelli, *The Prince* (New York: Alfred A. Knopf, 1992)

[2] Ibid.

[3] Ibid.

[4] Ford, Henry, *My Life and Work: An Autobiography of Henry Ford* (BN Publishing, 2008)

Chapter 10

[1] Drucker, Peter F., *The Effective Executive* (New York: Harper & Row, 1985)

INDEX

accountability 78, 81, 183, 201, 207
answer man 22-23
answer-provider 21-23
anger 8, 67
Art of War, The 85, 93, 203
assumptions 21, 23-24, 29, 32, 46, 105,
107, 110, 120, 130, 132
authority 11, 16, 23, 29, 39, 49, 51, 72,
76, 79, 82, 147, 171, 183, 186,
193-194, 196, 200, 203, 208-209
*Autobiography of Benjamin Franklin,
The* 37
Autonomy 40, 44, 48-49, 51-56, 66,
119, 124, 131, 180, 182, 185, 188-
189, 191-194, 206, 211-215

Bacon, Francis 7
Bias of Priene 20
big man 187, 188, 191
bottleneck 3, 188
bottom-up 21, 29, 48, 51, 100, 118,
189, 194, 218
Bridge on the River Kwai, The 137

call to adventure 94
Capabilities 4, 40, 47-48, 51, 54-55,
61, 64, 88, 119, 122, 130, 139-
142, 144, 151-152, 158-159, 161,
163, 165-169, 177, 210, 212
Capabilities-Responsibilities Interface
Capacity 4, 43, 48, 51, 54, 66, 88, 130,
159, 163-167, 177-178

CHALLENGE 17, 42-43, 48, 52, 87-96,
99, 101-102, 104, 106, 109, 112,
118, 120, 122-124, 129-130, 136,
148, 152, 160, 162-165, 169, 171-
172, 175, 180, 189, 192-193, 196,
211-214, 219
Chance 24, 30, 43, 46, 50, 89-90, 98,
103-106, 112, 117-118, 120, 123,
127, 129, 133, 144, 160, 162, 176,
181, 192, 200, 211-212, 214, 218
charisma 183, 195
Cheng and Ch'i 93-94
Churchill, Winston 20
cognizant 29, 31, 106, 108, 118, 189
command-and-control 5-6, 9, 61, 119,
147
commercialization 121-122
communication 44, 50, 55, 71-75, 81,
110, 195, 207
competency 161-162, 177, 209, 215,
218
confidence/self-confidence 15, 19, 54,
65, 67, 95-97, 99, 105, 112-113,
127, 131, 143, 158-159, 180, 183-
184, 190-192, 195, 211, 221
Count of Monte Cristo, The 1
Creativity 7,8,11,17, 24, 28, 43, 46, 49-
50, 67-68, 71, 89-92, 95, 104, 106,
111, 115, 118, 122-124, 127-128,
130, 132-134, 136, 144, 160, 162,
176, 181, 186, 189, 192, 195-196,
209, 211-214, 218, 223

ABOUT THE AUTHOR

Randall P. Vendetti, P.E. is Principal of Techne Synergies LLC, a consulting firm in engineering management and product development. He has worked in business and industry leading to positions as department head of engineering for a number of capital equipment manufacturers. He is a licensed professional engineer, holds a BS in mechanical engineering degree from Fairleigh Dickinson University and an Executive Master of Technology Management (EMTM) degree from Stevens Institute of Technology.

Randall would appreciate comments. He can be reached by email at rpvendetti@technesynergies.com.

Workshops based on this book are available for individuals at various locations and for organizations in-house. To learn more, visit www.technesynergies.com.